"Loori's handsome and practical book will find crossover audiences from self-helpers and artists of all stripes." —*Booklist*

"We don't know that we are already what we are trying to be'. This sentence, from Loori-roshi's new book can stop time. Ponder the 'we,' the 'know,' and the 'be' deeply enough and life will begin to reflect the freedom, spontaneity, and simplicity which Loori identifies as the hallmark of Zen art. He has managed somehow, to fuse the best of art and the deepest realms of ordinary existence in a way that makes illuminated sense of both. As a practicing artist and Zen student, I loved this book. Its achievement is that a mechanic could too."

—Peter Coyote, actor/writer

"With consummate honesty, grace, and humor, John Daido Loori shows us how art making and spiritual practice are inseparable; each informs the other, ripening the precious moments of our lives. Embedded in his eloquent writing are delicious and inspiring photos, drawings and quotations by a wide range of creators, from Zen Master Dogen to Leonardo Da Vinci, Carl Sagan, and Walt Whitman. *The Zen of Creativity* is a vibrant and essential book."

—Meredith Monk, composer/director/performer

"This is a powerful book. Daido Loori has given himself over to it and thus to us completely. Giving yourself over to it, you may lose yourself, to great benefit and illumination. Giving yourself over to it, you may find yourself, to great benefit and illumination. These are not necessarily different. It is worth giving yourself completely. Why hold anything back? The author hasn't, and as a consequence, there is no end to this book's riches, reflecting your beauty and creativity. That is some artistry! And also, as you will see, no big deal. Merely everything." —Jon Kabat-Zinn, author of *Coming to Our Senses,*
Full Catastrophe Living, and *Wherever You Go, There You Are*

"Artists and soul-searchers will find this book satisfying." —*Library Journal*

ALSO BY JOHN DAIDO LOORI

The Eight Gates of Zen: A Program of Zen Training

Riding the Ox Home: Stages on the Path to Enlightenment

The Zen of Creativity

Ballantine Books

New York

The Zen of Creativity

Cultivating Your Artistic Life

John Daido Loori

2005 Ballantine Books Trade Paperback Edition

Copyright © 2004 by Dharma Communications

Published in the United States by Ballantine Books, an imprint of The Random House
Publishing Group, a division of Random House, Inc., New York.

BALLANTINE and colophon are trademarks of Random House, Inc.

Originally published in hardcover in the United States by Ballantine Books, an imprint of
The Random House Publishing Group, a division of Random House, Inc., in 2004.

Grateful acknowledgment is made to John Hawkins & Associates: "That" from *Women
Whose Lives Are Food, Men Whose Lives Are Money* by Joyce Carol Oates. Copyright © 1978
by *The Ontario Review.* Reprinted by permission of John Hawkins & Associates, Inc., and
Joyce Carol Oates.

Excerpt from the Introduction by D. T. Suzuki from *Zen and the Art of Archery* by Eugene
Herrigel. Reprinted courtesy of Pantheon Books, a division of Random House, Inc.

Excerpt from *Zenga: Brushstrokes of Enlightenment* by John Stevens. Copyright © 1999 by
New Orleans Museum of Art. Reprinted courtesy of New Orleans Museum of Art.

Quotation by Minor White published by permission of the Minor White Archive,
Princeton University Art Museum. Copyright © 2004 by the Trustees of Princeton
University.

By permission of Steven Heine, *Zen Poetry of Dogen: Verses from the Mountain of Eternal Peace*
(Tuttle, 1997).

Soen Nakagawa's poems have been reprinted with permission of Eido Shimano, Roshi, and
the Zen Studies Society.

Library of Congress Control Number: 2004098821

ISBN 978-0-345-46633-4

www.ballantinebooks.com

Text design by Ralph L. Fowler

146122990

Come said the muse,
Sing me a song no poet yet has chanted,
Sing me the universal.

In this broad earth of ours,
Amid the measureless grossness and the slag,
Enclosed and safe within its central heart,
Nestles the seed perfection.

WALT WHITMAN

Contents

Acknowledgments

It's difficult for me to imagine creating a book without a cadre of bright, enthusiastic people for support. I have been blessed with a very special team that enabled the shaping of a manuscript out of my many years of teaching "Zen and Creativity."

Principal among them has been Bonnie Myotai Treace, who provided me with a magic mirror that helped me better see and feel the reader.

My gratitude also to my day-to-day team of editors, Konrad Ryushin Marchaj and Vanessa Zuisei Goddard and Kenny Wapner, whose language skills and commitment to this project helped bring my words to the page without ever losing track of my voice. And to Chris Trevelyan, for his invaluable graphic assistance in preparing the images for publication.

Finally, I extend my thanks to all the students and friends who provided proofreading and important feedback during the long journey from conception to completion.

Introduction

The arts of Zen are not intended for utilitarian
purposes, or for purely aesthetic enjoyment,
but are meant to train the mind, indeed,
to bring it into contact with ultimate reality.

D. T. SUZUKI

Creativity is our birthright. It is an integral part of being human, as basic as walking, talking, and thinking. Throughout our evolution as a species, it has sparked innovations in science, beauty in the arts, and revelation in religion. Every human life contains its seeds and is constantly manifesting it, whether we're building a sand castle, preparing Sunday dinner, painting a canvas, walking through the woods, or programming a computer.

The creative process, like a spiritual journey, is intuitive, non-linear, and experiential. It points us toward our essential nature, which is a reflection of the boundless creativity of the universe.

Zen Buddhism and, particularly, the Zen arts are a rich source of teachings to help us understand and cultivate our creativity. Zen has become part of our popular culture, but the arts of Zen have yet to make a significant impact on the West. There are only a handful of books in English that deal with the Zen arts and most are no longer in print. The Zen arts contain a treasure house of techniques and insight into the creative process. And they point to a way of living that is simple, spontaneous, and vital. They profoundly impacted an entire culture in Asia but remain essentially untapped in the West.

This book is an introduction to the Zen arts, and an invitation to explore them as a way to help you live a more creative life. It is not a book about art history, art appreciation, or art theory. It will not teach you how to become a better artist, or how to sell your art. Hopefully, it will give you an appreciation of the Zen aesthetic and the power of creativity to affect both your art and the day-to-day encounters of your life.

Buddhism traces its history to its original teacher, Shakyamuni Buddha, who lived 2,500 years ago in India. The Buddha, upon his own enlightenment, saw that each and every being, as well as the great earth itself, is perfect and complete, lacking nothing. He pointed out that our idea of a separate, limited self is a painful delusion. The self is empty of any intrinsic characteristics. All the Buddhist teachings are skillful means to help people discover these truths for themselves.

When Buddhism first arrived in China from India during the first century, c.e., it encountered Confucianism and Taoism, China's indigenous religions. From the second to sixth centuries, the elaborate, richly textured metaphysics of Indian Buddhist thought came face-to-face with the earthy pragmatism of Chinese culture. Indian Buddhism—replete with long lists of meditative states, elaborate practices, and a whole host of deities, demons, and other celestial creatures—was imbued with Taoism's accent on simplicity and its deep appreciation of nature and the arts. These traits tempered Indian Buddhism's philosophical tendencies. The result was the very direct and practical kind of Buddhism—Zen.

In the sixth century C.E., Bodhidharma, considered to be the first ancestor of the Zen lineage, put forth the four points that define Zen:

Zen is a special transmission outside the scriptures,
With no reliance on words and letters.
A direct pointing to the human mind,
And the realization of enlightenment.

Zen is about the experience of Buddha's enlightenment, not the words and ideas that describe it. To understand or believe in enlightenment doesn't impart any lasting strength. But to realize it—to make it real for yourself—can transform your life. The teachings of Zen always point directly to the inherent perfection of each one of us. The Zen arts are a form of that direct pointing.

During its early history, Zen was influenced by the refined practices of Chinese poetry, painting, and calligraphy. *The Tao of Painting*, a book written around 500 C.E., is a classic canon on the art of painting as a spiritual path. In the action of no-action (*wu-wei*), a cardinal aspect of the true creative process is set forth. In wu-wei, the mind is silenced and the work is allowed to express itself.

Taoist teachers often communicated their spiritual understanding with painting and verse, and the Zen monks who followed Bodhidharma took up this tradition. The Taoist approach to art was singular; it was centered on an intimate connection between a teacher and a student. *The Tao of Painting* talks about artists apprenticing with masters to learn how to discover and express the energy, or *chi* (Japanese *ki*), of a mountain, bamboo, or a plum blossom. Zen borrowed from these teachings to develop particular styles of painting, calligraphy, and poetry. The early Chinese Zen masters wrote their religious insights in the verse style of Laozi and Zhuangzi and other early Taoist sages.

By the Sung dynasty in China (960–1279 C.E.), the Zen arts of painting and poetry reached their highest stage of development, with the emergence of a novel phenomenon: painter-priests and poet-priests who produced art that broke with all forms of religious and secular art. This art was not representational or iconographic. It did not inspire faith or facilitate liturgy or contemplation. It did not function to deepen the devotees' experience of religion. It was not used in worship ceremonies or as a part of prayer. Its only purpose was to point to the nature of reality. It suggested a new way of seeing, and a new way of being that cut to the core of what it meant to be human and fully alive. Zen art, as sacred art, touched artists and audiences deeply, expressed the ineffable, and helped to transform the way we see ourselves in the world.

Zen masters began to use art as a way of teaching the *buddhadharma* (the Buddhist teaching) to both monks and laity. The monasteries became magnets for secular artists who were interested in clarifying the relationship between the deepest spiritual yearnings and creativity.

When Chinese Zen first traveled to Japan in the thirteenth century, the arts followed and became quickly integrated into the culture. The ground for this integration of the Zen arts was partially prepared during the Heian period (794–1185 C.E.) when the courtesans of Japan created an artistic legacy that later became the foundation for the Zen aesthetic.

These brilliant women artists originated spontaneous verse, a poetic form that eventually developed into haiku, the pithy three-line poem that has become so identified with Zen. The poetry of the courtesans had many of the traits already present in the Taoist-inflected Zen art of China's Golden Age—a deep appreciation of nature and a keen awareness of the evanescence of life. But the courtesans further refined the Taoist influences and gave their artistic expression a distinctly Japanese flavor.

In the Japanese art of this period we see the emergence of *wabi, sabi, aware,* and *yugen*—qualities that have become synonymous with the Zen aesthetic. *Wabi* is a sense of loneliness or solitude. *Sabi* is the suchness of ordinary objects, the basic, unmistakable uniqueness of a thing in and of itself. *Aware* is a feeling of nostalgia, a longing for the past. *Yugen* is mystery, the hidden, ineffable dimensions of reality.

Between 1200 and 1350, as the Japanese capital and the center of cultural activities moved from Nara to Kamakura, the Zen aesthetic blossomed into what we now recognize as the traditional Zen arts. As had happened in China, Japanese artist-priests began to build a reputation for their innovative style and the way they used their paintings and poetry to express their religious understanding. Although they were not trained artists, many of the abbots and monks that made up the orders of the great monasteries were renowned calligraphers, poets, painters, and musicians. Art practice was intimately woven into the fabric of Zen training. Zen arts, creativity, and realized spirituality were seen as inseparable, and a Zen aesthetic developed which expressed eternal truths about the nature of reality and our place in the universe.

As a teaching vehicle for the Zen masters in Japan, these arts—tea ceremony, bamboo flute, landscape gardening, Noh drama, ceramic arts, and archery—became known as the "artless arts of Zen." They transcended technique and were primarily used as tools for communicating spiritual insight. Paintings and calligraphy functioned as visual discourses. Poetry was used to create "live words" to communicate the essential wordlessness of Zen.

The most interesting aspect of these arts of Zen, as D. T. Suzuki has said, is that they don't exist for the sole purpose of creating a work of art, but they are rather a method for opening the creative process. They comprise means of training the mind and of living our lives.

In *chado,* the way of tea; *shodo,* the way of the brush; *kado,* the way of the flower, and *kyudo,* the way of the bow, the suffix "do" means "way." These arts were called ways because they were disciplines or paths of polishing the artist's understanding of him or herself and the nature of reality.

Since the teachings of the artless arts are passed down from generation to generation directly, mind to mind, the role of the teacher is pivotal. Before these teachings can even begin, a bond between the teacher and student must form. A teacher must have the student's permission to teach and the student must be ready to receive.

In the West, we learn mostly through explanations and specific instructions. In Zen and its arts, space is created for the process of discovery to take place. They are primarily taught through "body teaching." The teacher becomes a tangible manifestation of the teachings. The students bring awareness to the moment and try to embody the example offered.

A calligraphy teacher bows to her students, lays out a sheet of paper, and slowly prepares *sumi-e* ink by rubbing an ink stone in a small dish containing water, until the ink has acquired the proper consistency. This process is a meditation for everyone involved. There is settling and stillness. The teacher moistens the brush in the ink and stands poised over the blank paper. In a single gesture, in a single breath, the brush touches the paper and the calligraphy is executed. The teacher cleans the brush, while maintaining her meditative absorption and attentiveness to detail. She bows to the students. The students then begin their work. The teacher moves among them, observing their progress, adjusting their arm or the angle of the brush. The entire process takes place, essentially, without verbal instructions.

Because this approach is not possible in a book, I introduce tools that act as an alternative to a teacher. When taken up with consistency, they can provide insight and guidance into the creative process.

Although *The Zen of Creativity* is broken into four sections, its connections and teachings are not linear. The sections overlap and amplify each other. Part One is the story of my own journey to Zen. It was impossible for me to enter Zen through the front door of a monastery. Yet I was able to enter the religious life through the back door of the arts, and gradually to trust my life to lead me where it would. As I was traveling, the path seemed incredibly circuitous, but I see now that it was the straightest course I could follow.

Part Two is based on the workshops that I've taught since the 1970s on Zen and the creative process. It presents *practices* to guide you to a new way of seeing and creating. This section is not about understanding these practices but about *doing* them, over and over again.

First comes instruction in *zazen,* Zen meditation, which is the bedrock of Zen and its arts. Zen is experiential, and it is extremely difficult to do Zen art or appreciate what Zen is all about without practicing zazen. After zazen, you will learn about creative perception, a direct, whole-body-and-mind, unconditioned way of seeing. You will then engage in a Zen approach to the creative process, which emerges from this fresh way of seeing, and you will learn how to work with creative feedback, a response to art that is experiential and intuitive, not critical. Part Two closes with an introduction to *koans,* the seemingly paradoxical questions that have been part of traditional Zen study. Koans are a potent tool to help you break through barriers that may be holding you back in your art and life.

Part Three of the book shows how the unique aesthetic of Zen functions in the traditional Zen arts, and how this aesthetic points to basic truths about how to live freely and generously. This section deepens the appreciation of the qualities that are embodied in both Zen and its arts—simplicity, mystery, spontaneity, and suchness. There are more practices in this section that extend and reinforce the teachings of Part Two.

Part Four comes full circle to the beginning. The journey—both creative and spiritual—is never over. With each step, with each breath, we start anew. This is the ineffable heart of Zen. It can be pointed at but not grasped. It can be practiced but not held. It is about the resolution of apparent paradoxes and contradictions. It is about the way the creative act expresses our inherent perfection and enlarges the universe by making visible the invisible.

The emphasis of this book is on the creative process—not on technical skill. The creative process is unique to each individual. It is unique to you. In reading this book and engaging the various practices provided, you will discover your own way of expressing yourself.

This process of discovery is the endless spring of creativity, always bright, fresh and new, brimming with life. Where it comes from is not too important. What matters is that it's already present in each one of us, waiting to be uncovered. Ultimately, engaging the artless arts means to see into one's own heart and mind, and to bring to life that which is realized.

PART I

The Crooked Path

How do you go straight ahead
on a narrow mountain path which
has ninety-three curves?

AN OLD ZEN KOAN

ONE

Melting Snow

All the way to heaven
is heaven itself.

In the fall of 1980, after I completed Zen training in Los Angeles with my teacher, Maezumi Roshi, I came to the East Coast with the intention of establishing a Zen arts center—a place where Zen training would be used as the vehicle for studying, enhancing, and cultivating a creative life.

The Zen Arts Center opened in Mount Tremper in October of 1980. Its main thrust was the practice of art within a Zen context.

Art had been a passion of mine since I was young, but its deep connection to my spiritual journey didn't become obvious until much later. I started photographing when I was ten, and by the time I'd reached my mid-thirties photography had become an important part of my life. While working as a research scientist, I began teaching photography part-time at a local college. Spirituality was not in the picture—at least not overtly. The first time these two areas overlapped was in the late 1960s when I traveled to Boston from New York to see a photography exhibit titled "The Sound of One Hand," by Minor White.

I didn't yet have any sense that art might be a doorway to serious and transformative spiritual practice, but something more than good technique drew me to Minor's work. Minor was a "straight photographer": he didn't manipulate his prints during the developing process, yet his images transcended their subject. Looking at his photographs, I felt myself being pulled into another realm of consciousness. Minor's work pointed to a dynamic way of seeing, a new way of perceiving.

My life has been the poem I would have writ,
But I could not both live and utter it.

HENRY DAVID THOREAU

One day in 1971 I received a letter from *Aperture* magazine announcing a workshop that Minor was giving at the Hotchkiss School in Lakeville, Connecticut. I took one look at the price and threw the letter in the garbage. A friend saw me, and she picked it up.

"Isn't this the man you're always talking about?" she asked. I nodded. "Then why are you throwing the letter away?"

"I don't have the money to pay for it."

"Send it in, John," she said. "Something will come up."

And, miraculously, something did. A month later a tax refund that I had completely forgotten about arrived in the mail. I sent in my portfolio, along with my date and place of birth so an astrologer could determine whether this was an auspicious time for me to do the retreat. With the acceptance letter I got the workshop's reading list. It consisted of three books: Carlos Castaneda's *A Separate Reality,* Eugen Herrigel's *Zen and the Art of Archery,* and Richard Boleslavsky's *Acting: The First Six Lessons.* Nothing on photography. What did my astrological chart or these books have to do with photography? At the time I was making my living as a physical chemist, and my rational, highly critical mind did not take well to these requests. But I really wanted to study with Minor, so I went along with what he asked.

When I arrived at the Hotchkiss School I saw that there were

sixty participants, ranging in age from eighteen to seventy. Minor greeted us as we arrived. He was a striking figure, well over six feet tall, with a flowing mane of white hair. He moved quietly, gracefully, and when he entered a space, he filled it completely.

This oceanic feeling of wonder is the common source of religious mysticism, of pure science and art for art's sake.

ARTHUR KOESTLER

The first full day of the workshop began at four in the morning. The sound of a bass drum moving down the hallway arrived without warning. It was pitch black outside. *How are we going to photograph in the dark?* I wondered. Drowsily, I dressed and filed outside with the others. We gathered on a grassy field and a modern dancer began to lead us through a series of exercises. Everyone was participating, including Minor.

I turned to the man next to me. "Why are we doing this? What does this have to do with photography?"

"Ssshhhhh. Just do it," he said.

I had paid hundreds of dollars to study photography with Minor, and I wasn't about to spend the week undulating in the dark! Furious, I stormed away.

Back in my room, I started to pack my things. Dawn was breaking, and the line of dancers caught my eye as I passed the window. They were spread across the length of the field. I took the camera, screwed on a telephoto lens, and began to shoot, feeling very pleased with myself. *They can do whatever they want.* I'm *going to photograph.* That thought perfectly summarized where I was at that time in my life: standing apart, looking at the world through a lens, like a voyeur.

After the morning session, a group of students led by the dance instructor came to my room to convince me to stay. "You're not giving it a chance," they said. "You're copping out." I could have defended myself, but I was moved by the fact that they even cared whether I stayed or left. And deep down I knew that I couldn't just walk away. I wanted so badly to learn to see the way Minor did, to photograph my subjects in a way that didn't render them lifeless and two-dimensional.

As the days unfolded I woke up before dawn, meditated, and danced with everyone else. We attended lectures and did various exercises. We didn't even touch our cameras for the first day or two. Then Minor began to challenge us with different questions that dealt with our way of seeing ourselves and the universe, questions that needed to be resolved visually.

One of these assignments was a turning point for me. On day four of the workshop, Minor told us to photograph our essence. "Don't photograph your personality," he explained. "Try to go deep into the core of your being. Photograph who you really are."

Who I really am? I was absorbed in this question as I walked outside and sat in the field underneath a sprawling oak. I suddenly started sobbing. I couldn't stop, and I had no idea why. Somehow, that seemed terribly funny, and I began to laugh. I kept laughing until I was exhausted. *Who am I?* That question repeated itself over and over in my mind.

Back in my room, I packed my 4 × 5 camera and a small backpack, prepared to stay out overnight in order to resolve this question. I set off for the nearby forest and began wandering. Minor's instructions echoed in my mind: *Venture into the landscape without expectations. Let your subject find you. When you approach it, you will feel resonance, a sense of recognition. If, when you move away, the resonance fades, or if it gets stronger as you approach, you'll know you have found your subject. Sit with your sub-*

ject and wait for your presence to be acknowledged. Don't try to make a photograph, but let your intuition indicate the right moment to release the shutter. If, after you've made an exposure, you feel a sense of completion, bow and let go of the subject and your connection to it. Otherwise, continue photographing until you feel the process is complete.

The state of mind of the photographer while creating is a blank. . . . [but] It is a very active state of mind really, a very receptive state of mind, ready at an instant to grasp an image, yet with no image pre-formed in it at any time.

MINOR WHITE

Minor's language was foreign to me. I had no idea what this resonance was supposed to feel like, or how I would recognize when my subject acknowledged me. I didn't know if I could feel a sense of completion, or what I was supposed to do to "let go." Yet, surprisingly, I was willing to trust Minor, and the process. Somehow, I intuited that I could do what he had asked. More importantly, I knew that I *had* to do it in order to answer the question.

Around noon I came to a beautiful gully and decided to rest. I built a small fire, leaned against a rock, and was eating my lunch when I sensed someone's presence nearby. I looked up and saw the elegant figure of a man standing at the top of the ridge, the sun glowing behind him. He climbed down the rocks toward me, and I recognized John, a modern dancer and one of Minor's senior students. I had been impressed with John since the beginning of the retreat. He would often photograph as he danced, leaping and turning in the air with a Polaroid camera in his hand. Like Minor's work,

John's photos made me realize that there were other ways to photograph, other ways to see that were not so rational or linear.

I invited John to join me and offered him a cup of tea. As soon as he sat down, I started jabbering about anything and everything. In the middle of my rant he abruptly whispered, "Listen! Listen!" In the silence I heard a faint tinkling. Intrigued, I picked up my camera and headed off toward the sound, leaving John behind. I soon found myself in thick, dark woods. A brook trickled through the mossy rocks. Light streamed through the trees; bright reflections danced on the water in the surrounding darkness. Enchanted by the scene, I stayed by the brook for an hour or more, completing several photographs in a slow, methodical, almost meditative way.

When I returned to the gully John was gone, and there was no sign of him ever having been there. The teacup was still in my knapsack, completely clean. There were no crumbs on the ground, no traces of him anywhere. It was as if our meeting had never happened—in fact, I wasn't sure that it had.

I packed up and continued my wandering. As the sun passed the zenith and began its descent across the sky, the light that filtered through the canopy of trees became softer and warmer. None of the photographs I had taken so far seemed to touch the essence toward which Minor had pointed me.

Again, I heard Minor's voice in my head. *Photograph who you really are.* I was looking at the ground, navigating over big roots with the heavy camera on my shoulder. I looked up and saw a tree standing a few feet away and off to my right which riveted my attention. It was an ancient hardwood with a gnarled trunk. Something about the way the light spilled over it drew me nearer. I approached it, bowed, set up my camera, and sat down on the ground next to the tripod, waiting for my presence to be acknowledged. I sat as still and quietly as I could, with my hand on the shutter release. Briefly, I wondered how I was supposed to know when to make the exposure. That's the last thing I remember.

Hours later, I realized I was shivering. The sun had set behind the mountains and the afternoon had turned cold. Somehow, time had vanished for me. I slowly rose, aware that something deep inside me had shifted. The questions I had been struggling with during the workshop—all of my life, for that matter—had melted away. I felt buoyant and joyful. The world was right; I was right. I didn't even know whether I had taken a photograph of the old tree, but at that point it didn't really matter.

I headed back to the school, for an appointment I had with Minor to discuss my work. He was sitting on the porch outside his room, waiting for me. Settling next to him, the list of questions I had prepared earlier in the week no longer seemed relevant.

He looked at me and said, "You had a good day, didn't you?" I smiled, and he smiled, too.

"What would you like to talk about?" he asked.

"Honestly," I said, "I don't have anything to say."

"Good," he replied. "Then let's just sit here together."

The days that followed deepened my appreciation for Minor and his teachings. Something had opened in me, and the techniques and activities of the workshop started to make sense. Minor was guiding us to go beyond simply seeing images. He was inviting us to feel, smell, and taste them. He was teaching us how to *be* photography.

As I was leaving, I felt an overwhelming sense of gratitude for Minor's teaching that I didn't know how to requite. When I said this to Minor, he simply said, "You're a teacher, right?" I nodded. "Well, then teach."

For a while this is what I did. I was very productive at first. I was seeing and photographing in a new way, and the workshops I taught around the country reflected a deeper understanding of myself as a photographer. But as the months passed, this new way of seeing and the feeling of peace that accompanied it receded, and my feelings of wholeness and well-being began to fade.

I tried to regain my balance by re-creating everything we had done during Minor's workshop. I read books on religion, spirituality, and philosophy. I stood on my head, ate vegetarian food, and meditated. I listened to the music that Minor had played for us. I kept coming back to the questions: What had allowed the world to disappear so completely when I sat in front of the tree? Why did everything feel so right after that? Why did I feel at peace? And how did everything become cloudy again?

Do not go where the path may lead, go instead where there is no path and leave a trail.

RALPH WALDO EMERSON

I then set out on a crooked path to find the answers to these questions, not knowing that this path would lead me to the mystical tradition of Zen and a new way of understanding art. But the first step on this path was to see if Minor could help me to make sense of what I was going through, so that's where I started. Feeling a little nervous, I gave him a call. Without hesitation, without even asking me for a reason or even pausing to think it over, Minor responded. "Come," he said generously, "we can have dinner and talk."

Minor's large two-story house in Cambridge was meticulously clean and sparsely furnished. It was sectioned into dormitories and studios for Minor's apprentices, including a state-of-the-art darkroom facility equipped for archival printing and framing. Minor divided his time between teaching photography at MIT and maintaining this apprenticeship program, reminiscent of the traditional way in which artists and artisans learned art from a master. The training was rigorous and experiential, an extension of what I had encountered at the workshop.

Minor and I sat down to talk, but I was too shy to bring up my feelings of loss and confusion. Instead, we discussed music, art, philosophy, and some of the exercises we had done at the workshop. Hours passed, and just being in his presence somehow helped bring me back to the openness I had so painfully missed. Later, I would see how he had readied me, once again, to see what was right in front of me. He helped me to return to a state of "not knowing," a willingness to trust what the next moment would bring.

Back in the hotel lobby later that night I noticed a poster for a conference on visual dharma at the Harvard Divinity School led by Chogyam Trungpa Rinpoche, a Tibetan Buddhist teacher. The poster must have been there when I'd passed through the lobby earlier that day, but I'd been too preoccupied to see it.

Various religious teachers were presenting, among them a Zen master who would demonstrate the "Way of Tea." I knew in my gut that I needed to be at that conference. This was my next step, though I still had no inkling where I was heading.

The Saturday evening conference brimmed with excitement. Three hundred people filled the hall, many of them graduate students from the divinity school, and other students and teachers of various spiritual traditions. The highlight of the evening for me was the tea ceremony conducted by Eido Shimano from Dai Bosatsu Zendo, a Zen monastery in upstate New York.

As the stage was being prepared with the tea implements, I found myself oddly charged with anticipation. Eido appeared dressed in full robes. I was struck by his precise movements, his strong yet graceful presence. He walked slowly across the stage, knelt on a tatami mat and presented a brief overview of the Zen arts, using an example of Zen calligraphy hanging behind him and a small flower arrangement. He then led us through a fifteen-minute guided

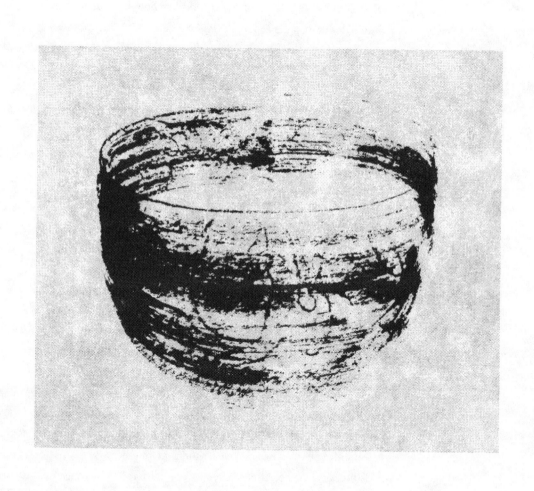

meditation in preparation for the tea ceremony. During the meditation, my body calmed. I felt relaxed, yet as solid as a rock. It was as if I had been drawn into a deep well, and a vast openness held me.

I watched closely as Eido prepared a cup of traditional powdered green tea. On the surface I saw someone simply preparing and drinking a cup of tea, but I sensed that the whole procedure had a much deeper significance. Eido's movements were smooth and unhurried. He added boiling water to a scoop of tea he had placed in the bowl. He whisked the tea into a froth, bowed to it, lifted the cup and placed it on the palm of his hand, rotating it two times. Then he said to the audience, "I drink this tea with everyone." He drank the tea in two sips and a final slurp. Then he carefully cleaned the tea implements and returned them to their tray. An assistant cleared the stage as Eido continued to sit in a meditation posture. He then opened the floor to comments and questions.

"I've tried to meditate, but I find it essentially boring," said someone.

"Boring?" said Eido. "Boring? What does this mean, boring?" People shouted out definitions. "Oh, oh, oh," said Eido, slapping his thigh. "I understand. . . . 'Boring!' " He began to laugh and laugh, so heartily that it became contagious. The questioner began to laugh, too. In a few moments, the entire hall was caught up in laughter. Then, abruptly, Eido stopped laughing, folded his hands on his lap, lowered his eyes, and became silent again. After a pause, he softly said, "Next question."

"I find myself agitated most of the time," said a young man, "so it's difficult for me to sit. What would you suggest I do?"

Eido reached for the pitcher of water that was sitting next to him. He lifted it with a swift jerk, causing water to spill. "What can I do?" Then he jerked the pitcher to the right. Again water spilled. "I don't know what is happening." Again to the left. "I can't settle down." Again to the right. Suddenly, he held the pitcher high above his head and in a deep voice shouted, "TIME TO SHUT UP AND

SIT!" and slammed the pitcher on the floor. He reared back, stared at the pitcher, pointed at it, turned to the audience, and said, "Look, it's still." Again he folded his hands, lowered his eyes, and became silent.

I was hooked. There was something in what Eido represented that day—something that I intuitively knew had much to teach me. I had a feeling that these teachings were the reason for my visit to Minor. They were behind my impulse to go to the Hotchkiss workshop, and they were connected to what I had found in the woods sitting with the tree. Zen fit in with all of this. I didn't yet know how, but I was sure of it.

Soft spring rain—
Since when
Have I been called a monk?

SOEN NAKAGAWA

After his question and answer session, Eido showed three slides of Dai Bosatsu Zendo while he talked about the training there. The slides were pathetic, underexposed, drab, and poorly framed. One was slightly out of focus. *This man needs a photographer,* I said to myself. I *could* have said, *I need a teacher.* But I just wasn't ready to admit that yet. Instead, I told myself that *I* was going to help *him.*

After Eido's presentation, I pushed through the crowd that had gathered around him onstage. I tugged at his sleeve and asked him for the monastery's phone number. I wrote it down, feeling with absolute certainty that the way had opened up for me.

Dai Bosatsu Zendo, literally "Great Bodhisattva meditation hall," was a three-hour drive from where I was living at the time. Pulling off the main highway, I followed small country roads that got narrower and narrower. I passed by the monastery gatehouse and proceeded up a very steep dirt road that wound through a beautiful forest to Beecher Lake—named for Harriet Beecher Stowe's family, which had owned the property. At the lake's edge stood a rambling nineteenth-century house. Up the hill, construction was under way for a new Japanese-style monastery building.

I parked and walked up the driveway to meet the head monk, who knew I was coming. He briefly described the lay of the land, and invited me to spend as much time photographing as I needed. That day I walked through the woods, following streams, circumnavigating the lake.

I returned to the office at dusk to ask the head monk if I could come back the next day. I told him this kind of photographing would take some time: several weeks, perhaps even months. I simply didn't want to leave. The monk said it was fine for me to come back and asked if I would like to join them for dinner and the evening period of zazen, or seated meditation.

So began a ritual that continued for several years. I spent three or four days each week at the monastery, at first photographing, and then, later, as part of the lay *sangha* (the community of practitioners).

One evening, a senior monk said that Soen Nakagawa Roshi, Dai Bosatsu's founder, had arrived from Japan. "Would you like to go to *dokusan* with him this evening?" he asked. By this time I was familiar with the language of Zen training, and knew that *dokusan* meant a face-to-face meeting with the abbot or *Roshi* ("old teacher"), so I said yes.

That evening, after the sitting period had begun, the dokusan line was called. When my turn came, I entered the dokusan room, prostrated myself to the altar, and stepped in front of the cushion where I'd been told Soen Roshi would be sitting—but the cushion was empty. I had no idea what was going on. I thought for a moment that I had walked into the wrong room. Still holding my hands palm to palm together in *gassho* in front of my face, I peered around the darkened room. "Roshi? Roshi?" I called out in a soft voice. Only then did I notice the master, sitting silently in a dark corner, watching me.

I walked over, bowed, and kneeled before him. He pierced me with his gaze, drinking me in.

"Please teach me," I said to him.

"*Namu dai bosa,*" he said in a deep, resonant voice. "Do you understand?"

"Yes, I do." I had chanted those words many times with the sangha. "Be one with the great bodhisattva." I nodded again.

Soen repeated, "Namu dai bosa. Now, you say it."

In a squeaky little voice I repeated, "Namu dai bosa."

"From the hara!" he commanded and poked me below the navel with a long stick that he had in his hand, the *kyosaku* or waking stick. "From here!" I repeated it, this time with a little more strength and resonance. "Again!" he growled. "Again!" Finally he relented, "Ah, good enough," not pushing me any further. "Namu dai bosa," he continued. "Every day, all day. Namu dai bosa in evening, Namu dai bosa in morning, Namu dai bosa waking up, Namu dai bosa going to sleep. Whole body and mind Namu dai bosa." As he spoke he reached down and rang his bell, ending the encounter.

"Namu dai bosa" embedded itself in my consciousness. I found myself following Soen's instructions as closely as I could. Whenever my mind was not engaged with something, it was engaged with "Namu dai bosa." I chanted it morning, noon and night, when I photographed, when I was agitated or scattered.

Early one morning after liturgy at Dai Bosatsu, I joined two other students to watch Soen create a calligraphy. Soen, an impish man of sixty-five, was a bit over five feet tall with a shaved head. He was always dressed in robes. Portraits show him as serious, even severe but, in truth, Soen was extremely playful and not just a bit

eccentric. One moment, his deep, gravelly voice would boom with great dramatic effect, the next, his craggy face would soften, breaking into the sweetest of smiles.

Soen entered the room, carrying a tray and a roll of sumi-e paper. He smiled at us and bowed, then spread out a long sheet, anchored the edges with small stones, laid out his brushes, and began to make ink. He added water to the ink dish and then slowly and quietly began rubbing the ink stone in the water against the rough inner surface of the dish. The ink stone, which is made of carbon soot held together with pine resin and compressed into a rectangular stick, is scented with a sweet perfume that fills the air as the ink is ground. Eyes lowered, Soen continued to work the stone against the dish.

The ink slowly thickened, finally reaching a consistency that satisfied him. He wet his brush and sat with it in hand, poised over a long, rectangular white sheet of paper. With a single smooth gesture, the blank space leapt into dynamic tension with the stroke of the brush. The second, third, and fourth strokes laid out characters. Each stroke complemented the previous one, activating the blank space around it.

*Where the spirit does not work with the hand
there is no art.*

LEONARDO DA VINCI

Soen diluted the ink by dipping the brush tip in water, and added light gray characters to his work. In the same gray ink he signed his name, in Japanese and Roman characters, and added his seal. He bowed to his painting, then to us. We returned his bow. I knew then that the path I had been following had led me step by step to this moment, this teacher, this bow.

> Snow of all countries
> Melting into
> Namu dai bosa
> SOEN NAKAGAWA

TWO

Mountains and Rivers

One of the gifts I received from Soen Roshi was a sense of how the Zen arts live in a person. He awakened in me a hunger to study how this art worked on the human heart, and how the tradition of the Zen arts might be translated into my own art and teaching.

Soen was not only a Zen master. He was an artist, a poet, painter, Noh drama actor, and the most recent embodiment of one of the most important historic lineages of the arts of Zen that went back to the seventeenth century. Soen was the abbot of Ryutakuji, founded by one of Zen arts' most significant figures, Zen master Hakuin. Hakuin is celebrated as the revitalizer of Rinzai Zen in Japan and one of the most prominent masters in the tradition of *zenga* (Zen painting).

Hakuin was the beginning of a long line of Zen masters who have passed down through successive generations the tradition of zenga as a visual way of teaching. Of all the masters whom I could have met in my early encounters with Zen, it was my good fortune to meet a holder of this long tradition of the sacred arts of Zen.

As I worked with Soen, I saw the living spirit of Hakuin re-flected in the many paintings that decorated the walls of Dai Bosatsu. Hakuin's powerful works of brush and calligraphy were charged with energy, yet they were still somehow tranquil. His art

spanned a wide range of subjects not usually associated with religious art: acrobats and animals, household utensils and courtesans. His calligraphy contained Zen teachings, quotes from the scriptures, but also nonsensical rhymes and quite a few jokes. Explaining a phrase of the *Heart Sutra*—one of Mahayana Buddhism's key texts, chanted daily in Zen monasteries—that reads "form is emptiness," Hakuin said, "A bowl of delicious soup is ruined by two lumps of rat shit." Yet Hakuin's art was never silly or simplistic. Even the most seemingly innocuous phrases contained a hidden barb, a piercing question.

Sometimes, Hakuin's calligraphy was direct, uncompromising. One calligraphy reads: "A single arrowhead breaks the three barriers," painted in bold, striking brushstrokes. It shoots the implicit question right into the heart of the viewer: *What is the single arrow that can pass through every obstruction, every barrier of greed, anger, and ignorance?* We can almost hear Hakuin demanding, "Don't tell me! Show me!"

As I spent time at Dai Bosatsu, I began to suspect that the key to the profound qualities I was seeing in Zen art was Zen practice, and that zazen—Zen meditation—was its foundation.

I had heard that as a young man Soen Roshi used to sit zazen high up on a tree to train himself not to fall asleep. It was said that once, when Soen was sitting at Dai Bosatsu Mountain in Japan (for which the monastery is named), he fell out of a tree and his head was pierced by a sharp piece of bamboo. Yet this incident didn't stop him from sitting.

During an intensive meditation retreat at Dai Bosatsu, I witnessed Soen Roshi's amazing capacity to sit perfectly motionless in zazen for long periods. I saw him sit through the day, into the night, and then on through the next day. Curious, I got up in the middle of the second night to see if he had finally gone off to rest, but there he was, still sitting in the empty zendo. Peter Matthiessen, in his book *Nine-Headed Dragon River*, wrote that when he was assigned to clean the zendo for work practice, he sometimes had to dust around Soen sitting in meditation.

Soen's capacity was extraordinary, to be sure, but the power of his meditation wasn't confined to the zendo, or the zazen posture. Soen's stillness when he sat was no different from the stillness that preceded his brushstrokes when he created a calligraphy. His every movement was poised, centered, completely present. This stillness and depth was also present in his poetry, which earned him the honor of being considered by many to be the Basho of the twentieth century. One of Soen's haiku reads:

Early morning,
Birth—
tiny dew drop, tiny plum

All artists are of necessity in some measure contemplative.

EVELYN UNDERHILL

When Soen wrote a poem or did calligraphy, I could see his whole being shift. He became very quiet, motionless, and I could feel the same stillness descend on me as I watched. Though what I saw in front of me was just a Chinese character, each time I felt as if the piece of art was all there was to see. It filled the universe. Soen disappeared, I disappeared. There was no longer any separation between the art, the artist, and the audience. It was a familiar feeling, similar to the time I had spent with my tree.

While I studied with Soen, I kept working on the slide show of the monastery, and when I finished it I showed it to him and the rest of the community. Millie Johnston, a wealthy art collector involved with various Buddhist groups in the United States, was in the audience. She suggested that I get in touch with Trungpa Rinpoche and offer to teach photography at his new university, Naropa, in Boulder, Colorado.

I was given the job and traveled to Colorado to teach a summer course. One morning shortly after I arrived, I was sitting out on the balcony of my apartment when I saw the university staff moving furniture into the apartment next door, recently vacated by a professor of Hinduism. One of the movers was carrying several Japanese scrolls.

"What's going on?" I asked him.

"The Hindus are out. The Japanese are in," he said.

"Who's coming?"

"Taizan Maezumi, a Zen master from Los Angeles," he replied.

When Maezumi Roshi arrived, I went next door to pay my respects. I introduced myself and told him I was studying with Soen. That evening, one of his senior monastics knocked on my door and said Roshi wanted to invite me over for a dinner of Kentucky Fried Chicken and sake. I went with him and discovered a full-blown party. For some reason, Roshi took a liking to me and insisted that I stay beside him through the evening. As we sat together, an unusual encounter ensued.

"Daido," Maezumi Roshi used the Buddhist name that Eido had given me. "Ask me!" He leaned close.

"Ask you what, Roshi?" I said.

Roshi turned his head away and was silent. Leaning close again, he said, "Daido, tell me."

"Tell you what, Roshi?" Again he turned away and was silent.

This went on for hours. At one point, I surmised that what was happening was a classic dharma encounter that required some kind of a Zen response on my part. So the next time he said, "Tell me," I lifted the glass of sake to my lips, took a swig, and said, "Aaaaah!" slamming the glass on the table. I looked at him. He made eye contact with me, and with an impish grin, pinched his nostrils together, turned his head away, and made the sound, "Phew!"

Some time around two in the morning I finally convinced him that I had to leave. I began cleaning up the mess we'd made, but he stopped me, said it wasn't necessary, and pushed me out the door. I was surprised and disappointed that a Zen master would leave such a mess, but I was also exhausted, so I let it go. I went back to my apartment and lay down on the couch in my living room, not wanting to wake my wife. I had barely drifted off to sleep when there was a knock. Maezumi Roshi stood at my door, wide awake and immaculately dressed in robes, his head freshly shaven. "Roshi!" I exclaimed.

"Come with me," he hissed. It was an order.

I followed him back to his apartment. The place was spotless. The low table in the dining room had four bowls and the implements for a formal tea ceremony. "Come," said Roshi, gesturing for me to sit down. "We will have tea."

He spooned powdered tea into a bowl and whisked it into a froth. "Soen Roshi," he said, placing the bowl before one of the empty seats. He repeated the process and put that bowl in front of the other empty seat, saying, "Yasutani Roshi." Yasutani was Maezumi's teacher, who had recently passed away. The third bowl he presented to me. Finally, he whisked one for himself.

The moment I touched the bowl to my lips and took a sip of tea, I felt something piercing, like a long skewer moving through all space and time. It skewered Minor White, Eido, Soen, Maezumi Roshi and, finally, me. I was so moved, tears of gratitude filled my eyes. Embarrassed, I glanced up and saw that Maezumi Roshi, too, had tears rolling down his cheeks.

I put the bowl down and through my tears watched Roshi as he completed the ceremony. Wanting to express my gratitude somehow, I stammered, looking for the right words, "Roshi, I—" He covered my mouth with his hand, grabbed my elbow, and led me to the door. "Roshi—"

"Sssshhh," he said. He gently pushed me out the door and closed it behind me.

For the rest of Maezumi Roshi's stay at Naropa we had no contact. I attended his talks, but he acted as if he didn't know me. The last day, when he was ready to leave, Roshi came to say good-bye. I bowed and thanked him. He looked past me at a scroll of Soen Roshi's, "Namu Dai Bosa," hanging over an improvised altar I had set up. He turned to me and said he wanted to offer incense to Soen Roshi.

"But it's only a silk screen copy," I said.

"It doesn't matter," he said in a gruff, slightly annoyed voice. He offered incense, bowed to the scroll and then to me. He left, and I stood on the balcony watching him, until his car was out of sight.

At the end of the summer, I left Naropa and went back to a farmhouse on the Delaware River, where I had moved with my wife and two-year-old son. Our future plans were not well defined, and with winter approaching, my wife began to worry. "Something will come up," I told her. "I'm sure of it. Maybe tomorrow morning after zazen, when we're quiet, we can discuss it and figure out what we're going to do next." I felt an inexpressible certainty that where I was headed would become obvious.

The next morning, at the end of our sitting, the phone rang. I looked at my watch. It was seven-fifteen.

"Hello, Daido, this is Maezumi Roshi."

"Roshi! What time is it there?"

"It's a little after four. I'm about to go to zazen." He paused for a moment.

"Daido, what is your relationship to your teacher?"

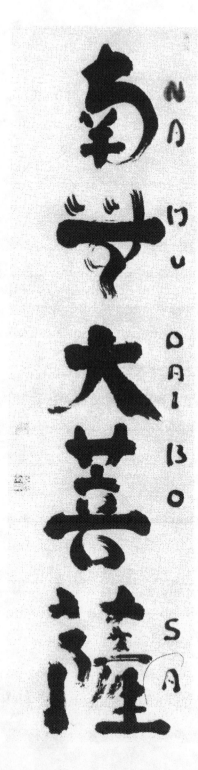

南無大菩薩

NAMU DAIBO SA

Surprised, I said, "I don't know that I have a teacher. I was studying with Soen, but he went back to Japan. So I guess I don't have a teacher. Why, Roshi?"

"Would you like to come to Los Angeles and study here?"

"Yes, I would love to. But we don't have any money, and I have a family."

"Let Tetsugen talk to you."

He put Tetsugen Glassman, one of his senior monks, on the line. "We'll pay for your trip," Tetsugen said. "And you can bring your family."

I talked to my wife, and soon after we packed all our belongings and headed to the West Coast. We left in the middle of a snowstorm and arrived at the Zen Center of Los Angeles before the December *sesshin,* the most intensive silent meditation retreat of the year. That was my formal entry into full-time Zen training under Maezumi Roshi, which would eventually lead me to become a Zen priest.

Moving to L.A. and studying in full-time residency with a teacher meant a major shift in lifestyle. The days were filled with meditation, morning, noon, and evening, the chanting of liturgical texts, caretaking the center's buildings and grounds, ritual meals, and frequent meetings with my teacher—in short, all of the attributes of classic monastic training.

The central focus of my teacher-student relationship during this time was traditional koan study, a device unique to Zen. Koans are designed to short-circuit the intellectual process and to open up the intuitive aspects of our consciousness. To understand the vitality of koan study, one must understand that the question, "What is the sound of one hand clapping?" for example, is not a riddle or a paradox. It's a question that has to do with the most basic truth. It's no different than the questions, "What is reality? What is life? What is death? What is God? Who am I?" These questions deal with the nature of reality. They are questions that every religion ultimately addresses.

At the time, Maezumi Roshi was working on a book of commentaries on the teachings of Eihei Dogen, a thirteenth-century Zen master. Dogen was the founder of the Japanese school of Soto Zen Buddhism and one of the most highly regarded masters in the history of Zen. He has recently been discovered by the West and is widely respected, not only as a great religious thinker, but also as a great writer and poet.

Maezumi Roshi's commentaries focused on Dogen's "Genjokoan" (The Koan of Everyday Life). I was asked to create color photographs for the commentary. These needed to go beyond simple illustration of passages and bring the teachings to life in a visual way. Isn't this what Hakuin and Soen did in their brush paintings? Can a photograph reveal the inexpressible aspects of the teachings of Zen in a visual way?

These questions became my work in the face-to-face meetings with my teacher. After presenting my understanding of a paragraph of "Genjokoan," I would express it with a visual image. At the time, I had little sense of how this work would ultimately impact on my way of understanding the arts of Zen, as well as my own way of creating and teaching these arts.

When we finally published *The Way of Everyday Life,* it was very successful and well received, so we decided to do a second book with another of Dogen's works, the "Mountains and Rivers Sutra." For Dogen, mountains and rivers themselves are a Buddhist scripture—a scripture that manifests the Buddha's wisdom.

When I began studying this sutra, it was an obscure text. The only translation available was a doctoral thesis by Carl Bielefeldt. I got a copy of it from the university library and started to read and digest it. In the midst of this work, Maezumi Roshi told me to go to New York City to assist Tetsugen to establish a Zen center. The book was put on hold.

"After you help Tetsugen," Maezumi said, "you can establish the Zen Arts Center you keep talking about." I had, for some time, been

contemplating using the arts as a way of getting people to appreciate Zen, and was hoping to establish a place for just such a purpose.

After about eight months on the East Coast helping Tetsugen, the opportunity finally presented itself to establish the Zen Arts Center. The building I purchased was located on a property with a mountain behind it and two rivers meeting in front. The auspicious nature of the setting reminded me of the "Mountains and Rivers" work that I had been doing with my teacher.

Although we say that mountains belong to the country, actually, they belong to those who love them.

EIHEI DOGEN

Soon after moving into the monastery, I picked up a copy of the *Woodstock Times,* a local newspaper, and saw, printed in bold type across the top of the second page, the first line of the sutra: "These mountains and rivers of the present are the manifestation of the Way of ancient buddhas." A page-and-a-half-long story on the "Mountains and Rivers Sutra" followed. I was stunned.

I immediately went to the *Times* office and burst in on the editor. "Can I help you?" he politely asked.

"How did you find out about Master Dogen?" I blurted out.

He looked me straight in the eye. "Doesn't *everyone* know about Dogen?"

He added that a book titled *Mountain Spirit* had just been published by a local press. In it was the Bielefeldt translation.

Following that incident, I began to study the "Mountains and Rivers Sutra" with renewed enthusiasm. I went back to it regularly as I encountered the problems and questions that surfaced while I

Zen Arts Center
Mounty Monastery
Mt. Tremper, NY
Graphite/ink/wash '77

struggled to formulate a way of teaching the Zen arts at the center. I was trying to develop a Western form of the Japanese teachings I had inherited from my teacher, particularly with regard to the arts as a way of making the teachings palpable to the growing number of lay students that were coming to the center. Many were jazz musicians, painters, sculptors, and poets, all intrigued by the relationship between Zen and the creative process. This was reminiscent of secular artists seeking spiritual guidance at the monasteries of Sung China and Kamakura Japan.

The "Mountains and Rivers Sutra" and Dogen's teachings kept resounding within me, and the early idea of the book that I had discussed with Maezumi Roshi began to re-form itself. I now saw the possibility of expressing the sutra as a film. It felt to me that the sutra needed to be expressed through visual imagery, sound, music, movement, and the words of Dogen.

I began working with one of my Zen students who was an acoustic composer and professor at Juilliard. We began working line by line with the sutra, treating each line as a koan in the same way I had worked with Maezumi Roshi on "Genjokoan." When our understanding was in agreement, I would express it visually, and he would write a score for it. We slowly progressed through the texts, wrestling with Dogen's profound language:

Because the blue mountains are walking, they are constant. Their walk is swifter than the wind. Yet those on the mountains do not sense this, do not know it. To be "in the mountains" is a flower opening within the world. Those outside the mountains do not sense this, do not know it. Those without eyes to see the mountains do not sense, do not know, do not see, do not hear this truth.

How could we express this visually? What did it mean to say "blue mountains are walking"? How could such a phrase be ex-

pressed musically? Line by line we worked to create a modern manifestation of these ancient teachings.

It became obvious that the music needed to return to the earth itself. A friend of the composer, a professor at the Manhattan School of Music, was brought into the process. He began recording the natural sounds of the mountains and rivers, the birds, insects, wind, rushing water, and he used these as the foundation for synthesizing electronic music that was folded into the score.

There are mountains hidden in jewels. There are mountains hidden in marshes, mountains hidden in the sky. There are mountains hidden in mountains. There's a study of mountains hidden in hiddenness.

The acoustic composer called on two friends who were sopranos at an opera company to sing Dogen's words. We were all pleased with the result, and joked about having created the first Zen opera.

The film was a success, and it went on to win awards. But the real success was the transformation of these students—the impact that Buddhism's ancient teachings in modern form had on their lives. The acoustic composer received the Buddhist precepts. I gave him the dharma name "Kyogen" (Source of the Sounds). Both he and the electronic composer entered a whole new realm in their artistic expression that was precipitated by Dogen's mystical vision. For me, it was the completion of the circuitous journey that had begun with Minor White and wound its way to the Zen Arts Center. The matrix for teaching Zen and the art of living a creative life had finally taken its shape.

PART II

The Creative Spirit

To study the Way is to study the self.
To study the self is to forget the self.
To forget the self is to be enlightened by the ten thousand things.

EIHEI DOGEN

THREE

The Still Point

Every creature on the face of the earth seems to know how to be quiet and still. A butterfly on a leaf, a cat in front of a fireplace, even a hummingbird comes to rest sometime. But humans are constantly on the go. We seem to have lost the ability just to be quiet, to simply be present in the stillness that is the basis of our existence.

The still point is at the heart of the creative process. In Zen, we access it through zazen. The still point is like the eye of a hurricane. Still, calm, even in the midst of chaos. It is not, as many believe, a void to retreat into, shutting out the world. To be still means to empty yourself from the incessant flow of thoughts and create a state of consciousness that is open and receptive. Stillness is very natural and uncomplicated. It's not esoteric in any way. Yet it's incredibly profound.

In zazen, we practice letting go of thoughts and internal dialogue, bringing the mind back to the breath. The breath slowly becomes easier and deeper, and the mind naturally rests. The mind is like the surface of a pond. When the wind blows, the surface is disturbed. Then there are waves and ripples, and the image of the sun or the moon is broken up. When the wind quiets down, the surface of the pond becomes like glass. The stilled mind is like a mirror. It

think
Non thinking

doesn't process; it just reflects. When there is a flower in front of it, it reflects a flower. When the flower is gone, the reflection is gone. The mind returns to that original smooth surface. A still mind is unobstructed. It doesn't hold on or attach to anything. At any moment it is free, regardless of the circumstances.

As we are liberated from our own fear, our presence automatically liberates others.

NELSON MANDELA

I was struck by the power and depth of that stillness when a student shared with me how he first learned zazen in Vietnam from two Korean officers with whom he served. It was, to put it mildly, an incredibly difficult period in this student's life. He was frightened most of the time, frequently on the front lines as a forward observer, charged with determining the exact location of the enemy so that he could direct the bombardments launched from ships cruising off shore. Shells inevitably fell short, exploding so close to his position that the ground beneath him shook. Sometimes his position was under fire from both sides.

During the bombardments he noticed something remarkable: When all hell broke loose, the two Korean officers always remained focused and calm. How did they do it? Why weren't they consumed with fear like everyone else? Finally, he decided to ask them, and visited them in their quarters. He arrived a little earlier than they'd arranged and found them sitting cross-legged, completely still, in deep meditation. He said they showed him how to meditate, and it radically changed not only how he got through his time at the front but the rest of his life. Something so simple as being able to be genuinely still—it's hard to express the great change it can make in how we live.

The still point allows us not to be consumed by the craziness that surrounds us, not only in the extreme situations but in our everyday life. So much in our culture now seems designed to agitate, and, in certain ways, we buy into it. All of us are conditioned, from the moment we're born to the moment we die. We are conditioned by our parents, teachers, nation, and culture. We live much of our lives as if we had no more potential than Pavlov's dog. When someone rings a bell, we drool. We find ourselves unwittingly living out the script that others have written for us. Or we react compulsively and repetitiously against it, still slaves to a script, but in another way. There is an alternative, and the still point provides it—to realize our unconditioned freedom.

> *The art of the inner work, which unlike the outer does not forsake the artist, which he does not "do" and can only "be," springs from the depths of which the day knows nothing.*
>
> EUGEN HERRIGEL, *ZEN IN THE ART OF ARCHERY*

The first step to access the still point is simply to quiet down. We are constantly talking to ourselves. We spend our time preoccupied with the past, which doesn't exist—it's already happened. Or we are preoccupied with the future. It too doesn't exist—it hasn't happened yet. As a result, we miss the moment-to-moment awareness of our life and barely notice its passing. We eat but we don't taste, we listen but we don't hear, we love but we don't feel. We spend our lives lost in our heads.

Living from the quiet of the still point means being in the moment, which is always right here, right now. It's very easy to say, "Be here right now," but it's very difficult to be actually present.

In order to get to the still point, we have to keep turning inward. We have to be willing to return to the moment again and again, consciously and deliberately. It's not easy. Try the following:

Sit comfortably so that you can close your eyes and relax, and for fifteen minutes, just listen without moving your body or mind. Just listen. Don't focus on any one sound, or follow any particular sequence of sounds. Let your whole being function as a 360-degree open sphere of listening. Don't process what you hear. Don't daydream. Don't doze. For fifteen minutes, please, just listen.

Most of us—seasoned meditators included—will find that it is very difficult simply to listen. We hear sounds and immediately name them, or we associate them with something else, we compare them, analyze them, or try to find their source. It soon gets boring just to listen and our minds wander. It's not easy to let things simply be and let go of our running commentary.

In Zen practice, we touch the still point through single-pointedness of mind, which we gradually build by working on our concentration. First, we count the breath: inhale, one; exhale, two, and so on. When we reach ten, we start back at one. When we notice the mind wandering, we see the thought, acknowledge it, let it go, and start back at one. Little by little we begin to build *joriki*, the power of concentration. Every time we consciously let go of a thought and bring ourselves back to the breath, we improve our ability to put our mind where we want it, when we want it, for as long as we want it there. And that is incredibly powerful.

The power of concentration is not just mental power. It can also manifest physically. Martial artists who tap the power of joriki can do extraordinary feats. One young woman who regularly visits our monastery is able to break two cinder blocks with her elbow. She weighs no more than a hundred pounds, and has an ordinary looking elbow. There are no calluses on it. She's not overly muscular. But her concentration is focused and intense. She can leap a solid six feet into the air and, with her foot, break two boards held by someone sitting on another person's shoulders.

The human form is absolutely magnificent when it is fully engaged. Most of us stumble through life using only a minuscule fraction of our potential. Joriki taps into our physical, mental, and emotional reserves, and opens our spiritual capacities.

One way that our spiritual power begins to manifest is through the emergence of the intuitive aspect of our consciousness. This is one of the reasons why Zen and creativity are so intimately linked. Creativity is also an expression of our intuitive aspect. Getting in touch with our intuition helps us to enter the flow of life, of a universe that is in a constant state of becoming. When we tap into our intuition, whether in our art or simply in the day-to-day activities of our lives, we feel a part of this creative continuum.

Single-pointed concentration develops our intuition. We become more directly aware of the world. We notice in ways that are not clearly understood, but are very accurate.

When the totality of our mind is focused on a single point, its power becomes staggering. Building concentration is just like any other kind of discipline. If we want to build muscles, we lift weights. Soon our muscles respond. To play the piano, we repeat the same exercises over and over. Eventually our fingers fly over the keys. It's the same with movement, with art. Repetitive practice builds our ability and skill. It's no different with meditation.

Counting the breath and coming back when we become distracted eventually becomes effortless. Then we're ready to simply follow the breath, to become intimate with it. By just *being* the breath, the witness disappears and there's just the breath breathing itself.

When you breathe in, breathe in the
whole universe. When you breathe out,
breathe out the whole universe.

KORYU OSAKA

In our daily activities, even small movements like the friction of clothing against the skin are enough to reaffirm the sense of a physical self. "Here I am, contained inside the bag of skin." But once we begin meditating and stop wiggling, that continuous feedback disappears, and with it the sense of a distinct self. Developing that power of concentration, we reach a point where we develop an off-sensation of the body during long periods of meditation.

This experience can be very disquieting for some. It's similar to what happened during the seventies in sensory deprivation tank experiments. People immersed in water that perfectly matched the temperature of their body would lose any sense of physical boundaries. For many, this was an intolerable experience.

During meditation, as we get closer to that complete stillness, we involuntarily sabotage it. The body sometimes jerks or twitches to reestablish its sense of solidity. But, as we become familiar with this off-sensation, we can relax into it. As the body settles into stillness, thoughts slow down. When thoughts finally disappear, the thinker disappears. Thought and thinker are interdependent, mutually arising. No thought, no thinker is called the "falling away of body and mind." This is absolute *samadhi,* single-pointedness of mind. In single-pointedness there is no observer. There's no awareness of time, self, or other. However, we can't operate a computer or drive a car in this state. We must keep going until this state gradually manifests itself as working samadhi, which means we are able to function in activity but from *within* a place of stillness, of cen-

teredness. When absolute samadhi appears in our sitting, before long it spills over into the rest of our lives, into everything we do. It's a way of being. All our senses become open, alert, free of tension, and receptive, but without clinging.

When you try to stop activity to achieve passivity,
Your very effort fills you with activity.

JIANZHI SENGCAN

In working samadhi there is no effort, no intent. It's 360-degree awareness; not so much like the awareness of a hunter, which is very focused and directed, but like the awareness of the hunted—unrestricted.

A deer moving through the woods will, at the crack of a twig, freeze in its tracks, filling its whole body with awareness. Its ears will twitch slightly, listening for sounds. Its eyes will trace the contour of the forest, looking for movement. Its nose will sample the air, scanning for scents. Then, if danger is confirmed, it will immediately explode into action to get away.

If working samadhi is present in your life, in your being, then it will be present in your art. Art always reflects the artist. If you're agitated, your art will be agitated. If your art is grounded in the still point, the self will be out of the way and your art will reflect its subject directly.

I once was given a great teaching by a friend, an internationally acclaimed clavichord and organ interpreter of Bach, on how important it is to integrate the attention and stillness we develop in one area, such as the practice of an art, into the rest of our life. The artist was also Maezumi Roshi's student, and on this particular occasion he had invited Roshi and me over for lunch.

My friend was visibly nervous about having Roshi, who was very important to him, in his house. He kept dropping things, and broke a dish during our meal. I felt for him and could identify with his awkwardness. To alleviate the situation, Roshi asked him to play something for us.

He immediately brightened and led us to the music room, where an ancient clavichord stood. He moved toward it, stumbled over the bench, and dropped his music. But then he sat completely still for several moments and held his hands ready to play. At that moment, he seemed to enter a totally new dimension. He was transformed into another being. The most beautiful and touching music flowed from the instrument, and we were transported to a place that felt absolutely sacred. When he finished playing, he sat for a second in the same stillness as we applauded. Then, as he stood up, the awkwardness returned.

. . . Even monkeys fall out of trees.

JAPANESE PROVERB

It takes work to translate absorption in an art form into the whole of one's life. One of the reasons the mastery of Zen artists—both ancient and contemporary—is not limited to art is that what they are actively addressing is something much more fundamental. They are studying the nature of the self and reality. How is that done?

From the Buddhist perspective, the self is an idea. It doesn't exist, except in our mental constructs. If you examine the question "what is the self?," the best you can come up with is a list of aggregates. My self is my body, my mind, my memory, my history, my experience. But those are aggregates in the same way that walls, ceiling, floor, doors, windows are aggregates that describe a room. They don't address the question of what is "selfness" itself, what is "roomness" itself, what is "chairness" itself, or "treeness" itself.

When you take away the aggregates, what is it that remains? Generally, in Western philosophy it is said that what remains is an essence: an essence of a room, a chair, a tree. Likewise, there is an essence of a self and, in the Judeo-Christian tradition, that self-essence is called the soul. In Buddhism, the enlightenment experiences of the Buddha and of thousands of Buddhist men and women over the past 2,500 years confirm that beyond the aggregates, nothing remains. The self is an idea. It is in constant flux.

Who you are now is not who you were when you were three months old. You don't look the same, think the same, feel the same, act the same. The same is true for you at eighty years of age. From a physiochemical point of view, there isn't a single atom or molecule in your body right now that was there five years ago.

So, what remains when the self is forgotten in zazen? Everything. Nothing is missing—except the barrier between you and everything else. You realize yourself as the whole phenomenal universe. Given this fact, then what is the self that is expressed in self-expression? Zen's answer would be that when the self disappears, the brush paints by itself, the dance dances itself, the poem writes itself. There is no longer a gap between artist, subject, audience, and life. This is not an accident or a chance occurrence. It is rather the result of personal training, spiritual development, and insight, which then manifests itself through artistic expression. In Zen, this personal training begins with zazen.

Practice: Still Point

Practice sitting quietly for fifteen minutes each morning, as well as every time you're getting ready to create art. In starting the practice of zazen, the first thing you need to do is find a correct sitting position for the body. Your posture greatly influences what happens with your breath and mind. There are several postures for zazen, including sitting on a cushion, a meditation bench, or a chair. For our purposes, we will deal with only one of these postures, called Burmese, because most people can do it. It's important to note that what you do with your legs creates stability. It has no significance beyond that.

Sit on a small pillow and draw the right foot close to your left thigh, allowing the foot and calf to rest on the floor. Place the left foot in front of the right calf so that both knees touch the floor. If you have difficulty sitting on the floor, sit on a chair, but be careful to keep your spine straight but not stiff. Be sure you're not leaning to the side, forward, or backward. Tuck your chin just a bit, so that your head rests squarely on top of your spine.

To get the feel of sitting straight, it's helpful to imagine briefly that the ceiling is resting on the crown of your head, and then let your spine begin to extend, from its base upward, as if you were lifting the ceiling a little higher. Be easy with this, and let your spine gently do the lifting. It's natural to have a slight curve in the lower back, so that your stomach pushes out slightly. Breathe through your nose. Lower your eyes, letting your gaze rest on the ground about three feet in front of you. Exhale, and consciously relax all the muscles in your body.

Now that you've established a supportive posture with your body, place your active hand palm up on your lap, with the other hand resting on top of it, also palm up. Let your thumb tips touch lightly, forming an oval frame.

Place your attention in the hara, a point in the body about three inches below the navel. This is your center of gravity, and letting your attention focus on that point can help calm the mind and create a sense of balance.

Breathe softly and naturally. This occurs spontaneously once you take the right posture, and relax into a calm attentiveness. Count each inhalation and each exhalation. Count one on the inhalation and two

BREATHE, YOU ARE ALIVE!

NHẤT HẠNH

on the exhalation, and just let the counting continue, following each natural movement of the breath until you reach the number ten. When you get to ten, come back to one and start over again.

As you do this, make an agreement with yourself: If your mind begins to wander, simply acknowledge that you've become distracted, let the thoughts go, and return to the count of one. This agreement is straightforward enough, but most of us find it pretty challenging, so try to be patient as you persist.

What often happens is something like this: You are sitting, counting your breath when, at the count of "four," you suddenly hear a fire engine go by. The instant you hear its siren, a whole chain of thoughts is set in motion. I wonder whose house is on fire? Since the fire engine is going up the street, the fire must be up that way. I'll bet it's the third house on the right. I knew that house was going to catch fire, it's an obvious fire trap. God, I hope those kids who were playing outside this morning are safe. Isn't it awful that people don't take care of their homes . . .

Before you know it, you have developed a full-blown story. You are a thousand miles away from your breath and posture, totally involved in this self-created, imaginary drama. When you realize what you are doing, acknowledge your thoughts, deliberately release them, and bring your attention back to the breath, starting the count again at one.

There are times when something so important may come up that you find that when you let go of the thought it will recur. You let go of the thought; it comes right back. You let it go, and it comes back again. If that happens, engage the thought and allow it to run its course to exhaustion. But watch it. Be aware of it. When the process feels complete, release it, come back to the breath, and start again at one. Don't use zazen to suppress thoughts or emotions that need to come up to your surface consciousness. Similarly, do not suppress thoughts of pain or discomfort. Thoughts will come up that you need to deal with. That's not a failure. Treating your thoughts in this open manner is another way of practicing.

In the early stages of your zazen, you may think that you are becoming more distracted than ever. It may seem that no matter how strongly you concentrate on your breath, you are unable to get beyond the count of two without the mind voicing an opinion or judgment. But your thoughts are not actually increasing; you are simply hearing your incessant internal chatter for the first time.

As your mind eventually settles down and your concentration deepens, you can just follow the breath, abandoning the counting altogether. Just be with the breath. Be the breath, letting the breath breathe itself.

In taking up this practice, keep in mind that zazen is not the place to develop your creative vision, write a poem, or solve a problem. It's a process that's intended to quiet the mind and to focus it, in order to develop joriki and samadhi. When these two elements mature, they will become working samadhi: the ability to be totally present with the subject, to get out of the way and let the art create itself. But keep in mind that this "letting" is not random or casual. It is a deliberate relaxing into the creative process. And the first step of this process is whole body and mind seeing and perceiving.

FOUR

Seeing with the Whole Body and Mind

Seeing form with the whole body and mind,
Hearing sound with the whole body and mind,
One understands It intimately.

EIHEI DOGEN

"Whole body and mind seeing," as Master Dogen refers to it, is the total merging of subject and object, of seer and seen, of self and other. This is, essentially, the experience of enlightenment. In "seeing with the whole body and mind" one goes blind. In "hearing with the whole body and mind" one goes deaf. And there is no way to describe this state of consciousness. The *Heart Sutra* takes up whole body and mind seeing by saying what it is not: "no eye, ear, nose, tongue, body, mind; no color, sound, smell, taste, touch, phenomena; no realm of sight, no realm of consciousness." But, as I said before, a person in such a state cannot function. He cannot get across the street without getting hit by a car, since he cannot differentiate between himself and the car.

In terms of spiritual practice, seeing with the whole body and mind is to "reach the summit of the mystic peak." This may seem like a profound achievement, but in Zen, this is not the endpoint. The journey continues straight ahead, down the other side of the mountain, back into the world. It is in the ordinariness of our lives that this intimate experience of the self merging with the absolute can begin to express itself.

Again, the *Heart Sutra:* "O Shariputra, form is no other than emptiness, emptiness no other than form. Form is exactly empti-ness, emptiness exactly form. Sensation, conception, discrimina-

tion, awareness are likewise like this. O Shariputra, all dharmas are forms of emptiness." It is not until we have reached the place where the absolute basis of reality is informing our everyday existence that the Zen teachings become alive in us.

This meeting of the absolute and its manifestation in the world is clearly evident in the classic arts of Zen created by enlightened masters whose perception of the universe is as Dogen describes it.

But what does this mean to the artist or practitioner who has not yet experienced this realization? How can any of us gain entry into this unique way of perceiving the universe, where every breath is the first breath, every sight and sound is fresh, penetrating the universe, reaching everywhere?

. . . Music heard so deeply that it is not heard
at all, but you are the music.

T. S. ELIOT

At one time or another, each of us has experienced this way of perceiving. It comes upon us unexpectedly. Suddenly the music moves into our being and our body responds. There is no thought, judgment, or conscious effort. The music freely passes through us. We pick up a brush and the painting flows from its tip. The poem creates itself, almost without effort.

Then why can't we live our lives in this way, unhindered, unfiltered? Why do we so consistently get caught up in our ideas, in the belief that we know exactly how things are?

All creatures experience the universe through the senses. And at every moment, a different universe is being created by each being.

A spider, for example, feels the universe through its legs, which touch the key strands of its web. It knows when it's raining, or when food is available. It doesn't think to itself, "That's not a fly on the web. That's rain." Yet it knows. The spider doesn't deliberate about what kind of fly it would like to eat or criticize the rain for trying to deceive it. A spider just does what it does, effortlessly and spontaneously.

For most of us, however, our habitual way of perceiving is not so simple. Our universe is filled with internal dialogue, analysis, evaluation, classification. We choose knowing over direct experience. Yet, in knowing, we kill reality, or, at least, we make it inaccessible. We live and create out of our ideas, out of the apparent comfort of certainty that they offer.

Plants and animals, for example, are categorized according to their biological classification, their family, genus, and species. That's the way science often functions. The multitude and complexity of life's web, all its myriad forms, are placed into useful groupings and subgroupings. Northern white pine is *Pinus strobus*. This pine grows all over Tremper Mountain near Zen Mountain Monastery. It's different than *Pinus resinosa,* which is Norway pine. Or *Pinus virginiana,* which is Virginia pine.

But what do these categories really say about the white pine I see each day as I come out of the front door of my cabin? It's been a friend for more than two decades. It has witnessed my comings and goings. I've watched it dance in the mountain's fierce winds. I've seen it shelter birds in a snowstorm, provide a branch for a red squirrel, feed a ravenous woodpecker. This tree, just like me, is an ever changing individual. It is easily recognizable from another *Pinus strobus* growing right next to it.

How many individuals do we miss in our daily experience because we've stopped seeing and started knowing? How much damage do we create in our confusion? James Watt, the U.S. Secretary for the Interior during the Reagan administration, said, during the debate over the giant sequoias in California, "What's the big deal about these trees? You've seen one tree, you've seen them all."

The poet Walt Whitman advises us: "You must not know too much or be too precise or scientific about birds and trees and flowers and water-craft; a certain free margin, and even vagueness— perhaps ignorance, credulity—helps your enjoyment of these things. . . ."

The less we know, the less we'll try to intellectualize our experience. Intellectualization closes many doors. One of the beautiful aspects of Asian poetry is the vagueness of its languages. Chinese and Japanese characters tend to have broad implications and multiple meanings that depend on how they're used. They don't pin things down as precisely as English does.

"Do," pronounced "dao" in Chinese, means "way," "path," "road," or "track." It's the character used in the various arts of Zen, in which it refers to the principles of mental training and discipline. In Buddhism, "do" pertains to the teachings of the Buddha. In Taoism, it is the first principle of existence. In Confucianism, it is the ultimate basis of cosmic reason. In Japanese, there are many other characters that have the same sound, which opens the door to various—sometimes amusing, sometimes profound—plays on words.

Besides this built-in vagueness, we must also take into account the fact that Chinese and Japanese characters are used in a significantly different way within Buddhism and Zen than in ordinary usage. Their meaning can be even more removed from the vernacular.

A professor of philosophy who was raised in China as a Buddhist approached me at the end of the morning service at Zen Mountain Monastery. She excitedly exclaimed that although she had been chanting the *Heart Sutra* in Chinese every day for forty years, it wasn't until she heard the English translation that she "finally comprehended it." The specificity and definitiveness of the English language allowed her to grasp the meaning of the chant. She might have understood it, but by pinning down the sutra's message, she was left with a concretized version lacking poetry, mystery, and spaciousness. Perhaps the experience was satisfying, but I'm afraid the sutra probably lost much of its subtle profundity.

This need to categorize, to understand our world, is an inherent part of being human. Take a simple object—a cup, for example. When I reach out and touch the cup, the moment my hand makes contact is pure touch; the sensation is unprocessed. But within milliseconds my mind needs to identify the object, and so the intellect kicks into gear. It sorts through its memory bank of previous contacts, just like a computer looking for a bit of information. Is it cold? Is it warm? Is it hard? Is it soft? Is it delightful? Is it furry?

Once we've identified the cup, the process of perception stops, and all other aspects of the cup are lost to us. We tacitly believe that when we've got a name for something, we know it. And once we know it, we stop noticing its qualities. We stop noticing the fact that it is perpetually changing and how it changes; we disregard what else it is. The art of attention developed in zazen lets us stay alert to the moment. It shows us how thoughts arise and interfere with our seeing. We can affect that process by letting go of thoughts and returning our attention to the immediacy of the breath and its pure sensation. We keep beginning, breath by breath. When that kind of attention informs our life, we see beyond our ideas into reality itself.

Practice: Direct Experience

The tea ceremony in Zen involves experiencing a cup of tea, but an important part of the ritual takes place at the end of the ceremony, when the tea master brings out all of the implements used for the guests to examine and appreciate. The tea bowl is presented as a unique work of art, without peer. It is examined by the guest both visually and tactilely.

See for yourself if it is possible for you to take up an ordinary

teacup and just experience its physical existence, without naming, an-
alyzing, judging, or evaluating it. Just feel it. See it. Touch it. Experi-
ence it without the mind moving. When you find your mind moving,
acknowledge the thought, let it go, and come back to the cup in the
same way that in zazen, when a thought arises, you acknowledge it,
let it go, and come back to the breath.

Usually we don't really look at anything at all.

CHOGYAM TRUNGPA

You'll find that the more you repeat this, the more you'll develop the
ability to experience things directly, without evaluation. You'll be able to
just see, hear, feel, taste, smell. And, as your attentiveness and awareness
increase with this practice, they will appear in other areas of your life
and art. You will begin to notice little things that you have been seeing
every day but barely noticed in passing. This kind of mindfulness is a state
of consciousness that is free of tension and focused on the here and now,
with no attempt to name or even understand what is being perceived.

An ancient Chinese master was asked for a teaching by one of his
students. The master mixed some ink and readied his brush and
paper. He sat in the presence of the blank sheet, then in a single
breath executed the character for attention. He looked at it briefly
and gave it to his student. "It's beautiful! But what does it mean?"
said the student. The master took up his brush, executed the same
character again, and presented it to the student. "Yes, yes, I understand," asked the student, "but what does it mean?" The master
shouted, "Attention means ATTENTION!"

When we truly pay attention, we see each object or situation for the first time—and it always seems fresh and new, no matter how many times we've encountered it before. We break free of our habitual ways of seeing.

Only that day dawns to which we are awake.

HENRY DAVID THOREAU

Suppose you have to work in a garden, picking weeds, and instead of the boredom and distraction that an inattentive mind would soon create, you see each weed as the first weed and the last weed of your life. You pick a weed—first weed, last weed. When you put it down, you let go of it completely. The next weed you pick is totally new. You don't know anything about it. You just pay attention. What does that mean? Attention means ATTENTION!

Practice: Caretaking

Create a simple practice for yourself using some routine task that you do every day, such as washing the dishes, sweeping the floor, or making the bed. Make an agreement with yourself to perform this task with total awareness. When you wash the dishes, just wash the dishes. As the Vietnamese Zen master Thich Nhat Hanh said, "You can wash the dishes in order to have clean dishes, or you can wash the dishes to wash the dishes." The same is true of any other task that we do almost mindlessly. Try bringing to it a mindfulness that is not critical, evaluating, or analytical, but focused simply on being present in the moment.

To practice attention means that when a thought arises, we see it, let it go, and return to the breath, to pure sensation, to the activity in front of us. That willingness to return to simply doing what we're doing while we're doing it is enough to open our eyes and let seeing happen. It is actually a radically different way of living. When we're not seeing, we get bored with our jobs, with our partners, with the day-to-day events of our lives. We keep inventing sports and challenges to keep ourselves excited.

Ordinary life has its own rush. We feel it when, being completely present, we step out into the world. There can be a rush in simply driving a truck or a bus, or digging a ditch, building a house, washing clothes, doing the dishes, but only if we don't blanket the unknown manifestation of the moment with our preconceived notions. We just allow each event to be what it is, entering it completely.

For hundreds of years Zen artists have continually revisited the same limited number of themes in their work, yet invariably, their expressions are unique, fresh, alive, and fulfilling. Hakuin's Bodhidharma is not the same as Sengai's. Basho's haiku are not the same as Ryokan's, though the two masters often wrote about the same subjects. In the art of *shakuhachi,* the same piece acquires a completely different tenor depending on the mastery, and even the personality of the artist who plays it. The ceremony of tea is made up of a very specific and deliberate set of movements that does not leave much room for spontaneity. And yet the process is different each time it is practiced. It is given a particular life by the artist who creates it and the uniqueness of the moment of creation. The same is true for all art.

Most people have seen photographs of a sunset. But of the hundreds, thousands of photographs of sunsets, maybe one or two will stand out, will really grab us with their force. Why? What was the artist able to capture in such a way that the sunset became unforgettable?

My own photography students often complain that their photograph of a sunset did not at all translate into the image. But, I tell

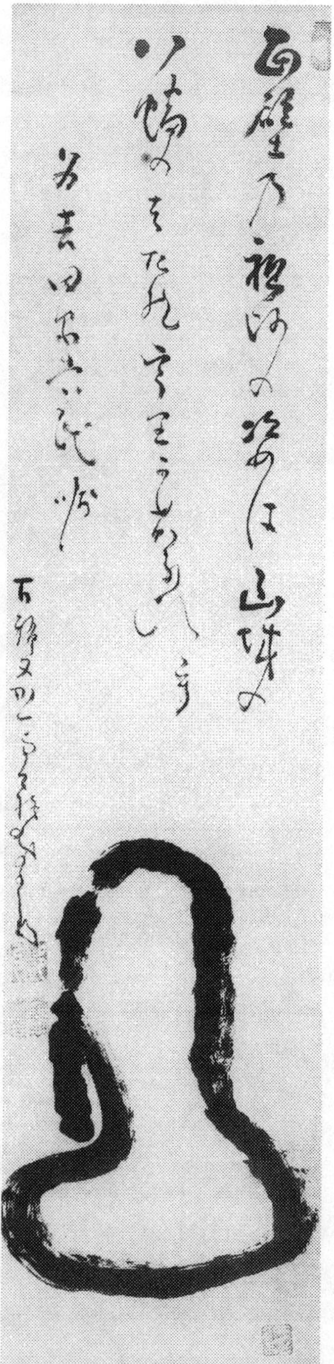

them, it's not that there is anything wrong with the image. It's just that they were photographing only one aspect of their experience: what they could see.

There are painters who transform the sun
into a yellow spot, but there are others who,
thanks to their art and intelligence,
transform a yellow spot into the sun.

PABLO PICASSO

We are usually only dimly aware—if we're aware at all—of the converging of information from our senses when we experience an event. We're so dependent on seeing that we tend to ignore what the other senses are communicating.

When we stand on top of a mountain, gazing at the sunset, we can clearly see the dazzling colors and shapes of clouds draped over the distant mountains. Yet, at the same time, we also feel the warm evening breeze touching our bodies, we smell the dampness of the mountain pines, we hear the sound of the wood thrush, we feel the cool earth under our feet. All of these sensory experiences contribute to our experience of the sunset.

It may be that we have to turn the camera away from the sunset and photograph our big toes, or some other image that evokes the totality of the experience of the sunset. This is not only true for photography, but for all the arts. The poet, the painter, or the composer who is locked into only the visual phenomena of the sunset may miss the heart of what was actually being experienced.

This is why whole body and mind seeing is so important. When we practice this whole way of attending and experiencing as we move through our daily lives—when we make direct contact with

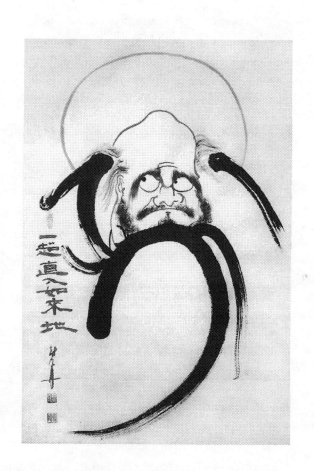

reality—we go beyond an ordinary way of seeing, of being, and touch the sacred dimension of our lives. To paraphrase Master Dogen: "In the mundane, nothing is sacred. In sacredness, nothing is mundane." Evelyn Underhill wrote at the turn of the nineteenth century in her book *Mysticism:*

> Contemplation is the mystic's medium. It is an extreme form of that withdrawal of attention from the external world and total dedication of the mind which also, in various degrees and ways, conditions the creative activity of musician, painter and poet: releasing the faculty by which he can apprehend the good and beautiful *and enter into communion with the real.* [emphasis mine]

Be aware that the mystic is none other than each one of us. "Entering into communion with the real" does not mean entering some kind of esoteric state of mind. It is *your* mind, right here, right now. To contemplate is to use your ability to see directly, intimately, and to express through the creative process and your life what you see—not what you *think* you see, but what actually is.

I shut my eyes in order to see.

PAUL GAUGUIN

Practice: Experiencing Without Identifying

Have a friend put five or six small objects that can be held in your palm into a small wastebasket. The objects should represent various kinds of tactile surfaces. Without looking into the basket, reach in and take one of the objects. Now spend ten or fifteen minutes exploring it with your hands, your eyes closed. Feel every part of the object, but avoid trying to identify it. As thoughts arise, acknowledge them, let them go, and return to the object. After a few minutes, return the object to the basket and put it aside. Repeat this process at another time.

You'll find that as you return to this handful of objects and examine them, you'll begin to develop the ability just to experience the object directly, without the need to identify it. You can then extend this practice to other sensory experiences, such as visual images projected on a screen or sound images. Try to develop the ability to just see, just hear, just taste, just touch, just smell, just see a thought (but without processing it) without the need to give it a name or identity. This way of perceiving will then begin to translate into the way you express yourself through your art.

FIVE

Enlarging the Universe

You are also asking me questions, and I hear you;
I answer that I cannot answer . . . you must find out for yourself [. . .]

[. . .] Long have you timidly waded, holding a plank by the shore,
Now I will you to be a bold swimmer,
To jump off in the midst of the sea, and rise again and nod to me
and shout, and laughingly dash with your hair.

I am the teacher of athletes,
He that by me spreads a wider breast than my own proves the width
of my own,
He most honors my style who learns under it to destroy the teacher.

WALT WHITMAN

Each artist expresses through art his unique way of experiencing life. This is the essence of creation. Through our art we bring into existence something that did not previously exist. We enlarge the universe.

If you wish to make an apple pie from scratch,
you must first invent the universe.

CARL SAGAN

The act of creation begins with the need to express oneself. Sometimes, this need builds in us almost imperceptibly; sometimes it comes on suddenly. It may be triggered by our senses, feelings, or even our thoughts. Regardless of its source, it can only be satisfied by giving voice to it—whether we do it simply with a groan of pain or an exclamation of delight like *yippee!* Art functions in much the same way: The creative process fulfills our need to express our experience. And if the expression has been true, we will feel a sense of completion and satisfaction.

Before engaging the creative process it is helpful to understand some of the basic elements that are functioning in it.

The first of these elements is the muse, a sense of inspiration that initiates the process of creation. The second is the hara, a place within us that is still and grounded. Then there is chi, the energy contained both in us and in the subject. Out of chi emerges resonance, a feeling of recognition between the artist and subject. Finally, there is the act of expression itself, where the expression is allowed to flow unhindered from the artist to the creation. The artist steps out of the way and lets the art happen by itself.

Let's look at inspiration first. It usually begins when our attention is captured by a subject, either a feeling or a physical entity. This attention draws us into the subject and we "feel inspired" by it.

In my own work, I have personified that sense of inspiration as the muse—a desire to express myself through art. The Greeks have created a whole mythology surrounding the nine Muses, sisters who presided over the arts and sciences. What I'm most concerned with here is not history or legends, but rather with developing the ability to recognize inspiration when it arises and learning how to nurture it so that it results in artistic expression.

No muse appears when invoked, dire need
Will not rouse her pity.

MAY SARTON

Next we have the hara. Central to zazen, the hara is also crucial in experiencing and cultivating this sense of inspiration. The process for allowing inspiration to clarify itself and develop into creativity is aided by cultivating a quiet space within oneself. For this, the practice of zazen is ideal. Find a place free of distractions and sit. Put your attention in the hara and follow the breath as it enters your body. Imagine it descending to the hara, then flowing out from it. As thoughts arise, acknowledge them, let them go, and return to your hara and the still point. Try not to define or pin down the feelings that emerge. Just feel them.

As attention settles into the hara, a feeling of lightness or buoyancy will arise. This is chi, the vital energy that is initiated by the source of your inspiration. Chi is power—not only physical power, but spiritual power as well. If a work of art does not have chi, it is lifeless. If words do not have chi, they are dead words, not what Zen calls "turning words." If our life does not have chi, it lacks vitality. The universe is filled with chi. If we do not have chi, then we have disconnected ourselves from the universe.

The chi of a being or an object is its spirit. It is the breath or living force that produces and permeates all life and activity. Chi is elusive. It can be sensed, but it is difficult to define. Ultimately, it must be engaged through intuition, not through our intellect.

The significance of chi is best understood by considering its literal meaning—"breath." In ancient philosophy and theology, breath, soul, and spirit were related concepts. The Sanskrit *prana,* Greek *pneuma,* Latin *spiritus,* and Hebrew *ruwach,* all have the same sense as chi. In Genesis, the Lord God breathed life into the dust of the ground and it became humanity.

Chi is the communicative link between artist and subject. During the creative process, our attention is captured by the chi that our subject emits. As we experience that chi, a resonance with that subject begins to develop.

In physics, resonance is the coupling of two vibrational frequencies. A classic example is the resonance between a pair of tuning forks. One fork is struck and begins to sound. When the second fork is brought close to it, energy from the vibrating fork is transmitted

to the second fork and it starts vibrating at the same frequency. The energy that is transmitted from one fork to the other is chi, and it can flow in two directions: from the subject to the artist, and vice versa.

Some of the practices that you will be asked to take up in this book will require that you get in touch with a feeling inside of you and then go out into a landscape to let resonance guide you to your subject.

Once you have located a subject that reflects your feeling, it's important not to rush into the process of expression. Wait in the presence of the subject until your presence has been acknowledged and you feel that a bond has been created. Whether it's a visual object or a sound, subjects change with time. They reveal different aspects of themselves if you're able to be patient and allow this revelation to unfold.

There is no place to search for the truth.
Though it's right beneath your feet,
it can't be found.
Look at springtime—when the snow has melted
the scars of the landscape are no longer hidden.

JOHN DAIDO LOORI

On occasion, I have sat for hours with a subject, waiting to release the shutter. As the light changed and my perceptive ability deepened, I watched one transformation after another. The subject kept displaying a long line of its faces, not apparent at the outset.

As you work with the subject you will find that the chi of the subject and its resonance with you will rise and fall. There will be peak moments and moments when the resonance is weak. Stay attuned and open to these shifts; use your intuition and respond by creating when the resonance is peaking. It is here that the expression begins, when you put the pen to paper, brush to canvas, or let the shutter release itself.

If the energy is really flowing freely, the brush paints by itself, the camera photographs, the sculpture forms, the words write, the dance dances. The creator of the art, the subject of the art, and the expression itself merge into a single process in which there is no reflection or evaluation, just the art manifesting itself.

A few years ago I went on a pilgrimage to Point Lobos, California, a mecca for artists who consider photography a sacred art. I entered Weston Beach—named for photographer Edward Weston—and descended into a bowl-like cove peppered with small islands. Little by little, layers of mental noise fell away. My impressions of the plane ride to the West Coast, the airport, city, highways, their sounds and smells, began to dissolve from my consciousness until there was only the immediacy of Point Lobos.

Then the dance began. As my senses cleared, images began to reveal themselves, gradually at first, then more and more intensely until they were rushing at me. I could not ignore them: gold kelp floating in royal purple tidal pools; wet rocks splashed with lichen graffiti; bone bleached shells resting on a bed of multicolored pebbles. Images kept appearing and disappearing, accompanied by the symphony of surf, sea lions, and the wind whistling through rock crevasses. I spent the whole day photographing as image after image appeared before me. It was all I could do to keep up.

In the creative process, as long as the energy is strong, the process continues. It may take minutes or hours. As long as you feel chi peaking and flowing, let it run its course. It's important to allow this flow and expression, without attempting to edit what is happening—without trying to name, judge, analyze, or understand it. The time for editing is later. The time for uninhibited flow of expression is now.

Every artist at some time in their life walks on water.

MINOR WHITE

As you continue to give voice to the experience through your creative expression, the resonance will slowly begin to ebb. The process will naturally come to a place of closure, with a deep sense of completion. That feeling of completion may be for a piece that is actually finished and does not need any editing, or for a part of the piece which will need to be returned to later for polishing. When that feeling of closure begins to set in, it's important to acknowledge it and begin stepping back while the energy is still present.

During that same trip to Point Lobos, I clearly felt when the creative process was coming to an end. As the sun settled behind the clouds just above the horizon, the wind died down, as did the sound of the surf. In the waning light, everything became quiet. I took a few last photographs intermingled with bows of gratitude. When I turned to walk away from the ocean, I was filled with a feeling of completion so pure that I did not need to look back.

When the creative process is complete, it is important to find some way of acknowledging what has just occurred. For me, this means doing a simple bow. Others may find their own way to express gratitude. Expressing gratitude is essential, especially if we need to return to our work and reawaken the bond that was initially created.

Most art is rarely completed in a single session. The photographer will have to reconnect in the darkroom with the feelings she experienced, the filmmaker in the editing room, the writer in rewriting. Where the original expression was purely creative, editing is at once creative and critical. By cutting away the extra, we get closer to the essence of what we intended to convey.

The editing process begins with reconnecting with the feeling, the resonance, that was present during the creation of the work of art. Then, we slowly and deliberately remove the unnecessary elements, without disturbing the feeling of resonance. If the resonance weakens, we've gone too far.

When I am editing a series of photographs that are part of a related theme, I pin them up on a wall that I pass frequently. I look at them casually, and with time find that there are certain images that leave a strong impression on me. I remove the ones that don't stand out. Space opens up between images that remain. Certain photographs will begin to pair, and I bring them together. The pairs begin to attract other single images or pairs, and little by little, a sequence develops that enhances the original resonance of the images.

This same process can work with the editing of other media. Attending to chi and resonance can facilitate the process considerably, particularly if the mind is empty and you trust your intuition.

After expressing our appreciation, a very conscious and complete letting go is pivotal—letting go of the subject, feelings, the process, and what we have created. This provides a fresh space for whatever it is that you are going to do next.

Ultimately, all of the elements presented above—muse, hara, chi, resonance, expression, editing—are really nothing but the self. It is important to trust this and to trust the process. Trust yourself. Your way of experiencing the world is unique. And what you're trying to do is give voice to this unique experience. Criticism in art is certainly valuable, but the creative process and developing your creative abilities is not the place for it. It is important, in engaging the creative process, to be able to work freely, without hindrance or judgment.

As you take up the practices below, be careful not to set a goal. Expectation precludes the opportunity for discovery. When we try to reach a goal, we become fixated on it and we miss the process.

Process and goal are the same reality. Each step clearly contains the goal.

I never think of the future—it comes soon enough.

ALBERT EINSTEIN

Practice: Expressing Things for What Else They Are

Having seen the many facets that exist within a subject, in this practice we will deliberately explore things for what else they are. This means we will try to make contact with different ways of seeing a subject. We need to not be bound by the names or ideas normally associated with things. Here we are dealing with the question, "What is real; what is reality?"

There was a Chinese philosopher named Zhuangzi. He dreamed that he was a butterfly and he was flying around and dancing. When he awoke from the dream, he wasn't sure whether it was Zhuangzi who dreamed that he was a butterfly, or if it was a butterfly that dreamed he was Zhuangzi.

This is an interesting story. Was it a dream or reality? Is this a dream or reality? To make a work of art that shows what else a subject is, you have to let go of your ideas and open yourself to see beyond the obvious or ordinary. This doesn't mean going out and photographing a face in a cloud. It means allowing the subject to reveal its multiple facets.

If you see a tree, do you see it as fuel, lumber, a staff? At different times, a person may be a healer, a lover, a parent. What is the reality of the person? What is the dream that Zhuangzi spoke of? This practice is designed to help you express that dream through your art, to see the dream / nondream, reality / nonreality as unity.

Go out without any preconceived notions about what you're looking for. Allow the subject to find you. Tune in to your feelings and let
the quality of resonance guide you.

When your subject has found you, sit with it and wait for your
presence to be acknowledged. Continue to sit with the subject and
allow it to reveal itself to you.

You do not need to leave your room. . . .
Remain sitting at your table and listen.
Do not even listen, simply wait. Do not even wait,
be quite still and solitary. The world will freely
offer itself to you to be unmasked. It has no choice.
It will roll in ecstasy at your feet.

FRANZ KAFKA

At first, the familiar surface aspects of the subject will become apparent. It may take some time for the subject to reveal its more subtle
and mysterious dimensions. Be patient. Be willing to be with your subject without knowing what it is, without projecting your ideas onto it.
When the subject shows what else it is, you will feel it in your hara.
It's not something for you to understand or name.

When you have felt what else the subject is, stay in contact with
the feeling and begin to express it in the medium of your choice. Don't
step back from your experience and judge it. Just let the subject be,
however it presents itself, and allow your expression to come out as
it will. Be intimate with the experience. When you've finished, thank
your subject in whatever way seems appropriate to you, and then let
it go.

In the "Mountains and Rivers Sutra" Master Dogen says:

> Thus, what different types of beings see is different, and we should reflect on this fact. Is it that there are various ways of seeing one object, or is it that we have mistaken various images for one object? We should concentrate every effort on understanding these questions, and then concentrate even more. Given this multitude of perspectives, it follows that the training on the way of practice and verification must also not be merely of one or two kinds, and the ultimate realm must have a thousand types and ten thousand kinds.

SIX

Jeweled Mirror

Many artists spend a lifetime creating, exhibiting, and publishing their art, yet never know how their audience experiences their work. Professional artists who have published or exhibited know what the critics think of their art, or whether it's commercially successful. But beyond that, do they really know what they're communicating? What are the emotions their art awakens? The same questions apply to anyone who practices art as a hobby.

Our art is always communicating, and we need to be conscious of what its message is. Creative feedback offers artists an opportunity to get a sense of the impact of their work: the visceral, direct effect that they're having on their audience.

It should be clear at this point that the process of quieting and focusing the mind is common to creative perception and creative expression. As we will see here, it is also the central element of creative feedback.

Evelyn Underhill, speaking about the mystic's way of perceiving, describes the following exercise.

Look for a little time, in a special and undivided manner, at some simple, concrete, and external thing. This object of our contemplation may be almost anything we please: a picture, a statue, a tree, a distant hillside, a growing plant, running water, little living things. . . . Look, then, at this thing which you have chosen. Willfully yet tranquilly refuse the messages which countless other aspects of the world are sending; and so concentrate your whole attention on this one act of loving sight that all other objects are excluded from the conscious field. Do not think, but as it were pour out your personality towards it: let your soul be in your eyes. Almost at once, this new method of perception will reveal unsuspected qualities in the external world.

What one seems to want in art, in experiencing it, is the same thing that is necessary for its creation, a self-forgetful, perfectly useless concentration.

ELIZABETH BISHOP

First, you will perceive about you a strange and deepening quietness; a slowing down of our feverish mental time. Next, you will become aware of a heightened significance, an intensified existence in the thing at which you look. As you, with all your consciousness, lean out toward it, an answering current will meet yours. It seems as though the barrier between its life and your own, between subject and object, had melted away. You are merged with it, in an act of true communion: and you know the secret of its being deeply and unforgettably.

Many years later, photographer Minor White applied some of these principles of intimate perception and contemplation in his photography workshops in a process he called "creative audience." In this book we will be dealing with the same process, embedded in the teachings of Zen and Zen meditation.

The inner—what is it?
if not intensified sky . . .

RAINER MARIA RILKE

It's sometimes surprising what happens when we suspend judgment and get in touch with how art makes us feel. I sat in a creative feedback session once where two young women, Cynthia and Rose, were working on a photograph of a beautiful rocking chair sitting in front of a window, with light streaming on it. Rose, who was giving the feedback, began to describe how the chair made her think of an old woman with arthritis in one hand.

"She's holding a cane," Rose said, "and she's wearing a shawl around her shoulders. She's also a bit blind."

While Rose was talking, Cynthia began to cry. Rose was describing Cynthia's grandmother, an old woman who had sat in that rocking chair every day for forty years. Rose had never met Cynthia's grandmother—she had passed away some time before—but her intuition allowed her to tap into the depths contained in the image of the rocking chair.

This is not an easy process. It requires a deep sense of trust between the person giving the feedback and the person receiving it, and it takes time and patience to develop this trust. Once the process is working, it acts as a doorway to insight. What we create in our lives can be a powerful teacher. A key element that enables this to happen is a creative feedback group. Members of such a group do not necessarily have to be artists. They can be peers, nonartists, anyone willing to look at your art.

In my own work, I have preferred to work with small groups. The group I used for years consisted of a couple of art critics, a photography teacher, an art student, a writer, the farmer across the road, and my mother.

It was very revealing to have such a mixed group since, even though their knowledge of and interest in art varied widely, the comments I heard from each were not that different. My mother, for example, never understood my abstract photographs. She would invariably say to me, "Oh John, you have such lovely children! Why don't you photograph them instead of these silly rocks?" Yet, her feelings about my work were essentially identical to the feelings that the critics and photographers expressed.

Part of training a feedback group requires that you be relentless in demanding that your audience express their feelings, not their ideas, criticisms, or opinions. Some people have difficulty getting in touch with their feelings, but you'll find that the process itself will help them to open up. It takes time, patience, and commitment to develop a functioning feedback group.

As the artist receiving the feedback, you need to train yourself how to hear what's being said and draw out the information that only the audience can give you. The tendency for the artist is to "hear" what he wants to hear, according to his preconceived notions of his art, rather than what it is actually communicating.

One of the pitfalls of creative feedback is you may find yourself trying to create art that pleases your creative feedback group, rather than art that springs from your own vision. Learn from your group, but keep going, keep exploring. Don't get hooked on looking for approval. It's easy for us to work hard until we master a technique, then just keep plodding along in a rut because we know we can work well in it. Take chances. Some of the greatest work has been produced by people who were willing to be rejected. Experiment.

Practice: Creative Feedback

For creative feedback to work, we need to enter into the still point first, deepening our attention until the mind is relaxed, free of tension, and focused on the here and now. Although you may have been practicing zazen and have developed skill in attentiveness, your group of volunteers may not have acquired such skills. They will need to be guided through a relaxation and focusing process before engaging the art.

What follows is an example of how this process works. Using yourself as the audience and the picture on the previous page as the subject, try this practice yourself. Since creative feedback is a guided, meditative way of experiencing art, you should either prerecord the following instructions or have a friend read them to you as you engage the image. The instructions must be given in a slow and deliberate manner, allowing enough time for each step to be engaged.

Place the image in front of you, but don't study it yet. Make yourself comfortable and relax your body completely. Begin by closing your eyes and becoming aware of your face, especially the muscles around the eyes. Become aware of any tension that may be there, then deliberately and consciously let go of that tension. Next relax the muscles of your jaw so it hangs loosely, gently pressing your tongue against the roof of your mouth. Now move to the muscles on the back of the neck; be aware of any tension there and let it go. Relax the muscles of the back, the shoulders, and the chest.

Become aware of your breathing. Allow yourself to breathe deeply and easily, without effort. Imagine each inhalation bringing energy into the body and each exhalation letting go of tension. If your mind begins to wander, don't fight it. Witness what it's doing, and after a few moments, bring your attention back to your breath.

Next let go of the tension in your stomach. Become aware of the muscles of the arms and let go of any tension that you may be holding. Do the same for the forearms, and the muscles in your hands. Feel the muscles of the thighs, the calves, and the feet, letting go of any tension left in your body.

Now imagine you are sitting next to a small pond. On its surface floats a white swan. It's very still. There is no movement. No wind. No sound. Try to feel that stillness with your whole body. Try to contact that still place within yourself that relates to the pond and the swan.

Turn your awareness to your hara. Begin drawing energy from all parts of your body to that point, from the top of your head and the tips of your toes and fingers. Focus all the energy of your body in your hara; feel it building there. Now begin to move that energy upward to the back of your closed eyelids.

When you're ready to begin, open your eyes, take a flash look at the image, and close your eyes again. Keep yourself still and quiet. How does it feel? What part of your body is involved in this perception?

Try to see the image on the back of your closed eyelids, and notice how you feel—not what you think of it, but how you feel. Fill in areas of the image that are unclear to you. Don't worry about getting it right. Stay connected with your feelings.

Now open your eyes and take in the whole image at once. How does that feel? Not what you think of it, but how it feels. See everything that the artist intended to present. Begin to move slowly through the image. Are there parts that attract you more than others? Sections that repulse you? Allow your eyes to scan every section of the image—don't leave anything out. Try to postpone your judgment. Just see and feel. If thoughts arise, acknowledge them, let them go, and return to just seeing, just feeling.

Now imagine yourself entering the image, becoming part of it. Be aware of how it feels from the inside. Are visceral sensations evoked by the image? Is it smooth, hot, pebbly? Do you feel nervous, excited, relaxed? Just keep seeing and feeling without judging or analyzing. Tune into your body as you move from area to area, noticing how the *ground feels beneath your feet. Is it spongy, smooth, hard, wet? Are there any sounds? Smells? Don't try to make sense of what you're feeling. Just let it move through you.*

Now choose a particular area of the image to go into. Become it. Notice how you feel, being this place. How does the rest of the image look from this position? Do you feel big, small, frightened, confident, weary, or angry? Notice any bodily sensations. How does it feel to move out of being this one area and back into the whole image?

What happens if you try to move out and beyond the image? How does the image continue beyond the borders? Do you feel relief, anxiety, fear, joy? Spend some time outside the borders of the image. Then return to the image just as it is, seeing it as a whole. Take it in all at once again, before closing your eyes, and again see the afterimage on the back of your closed eyelids. Fill in any areas that aren't clear. Notice the sensations you are left with. Try to amplify the feeling and really experience it. Then let it go.

Draw your energy back down to your hara and away from your eyes. Feel the energy building there until you feel that sense of lightness, warmth, or buoyancy. Then consciously and deliberately let it go. Let go of the feeling; let go of the image. Become aware of yourself, the room, and sounds. Move your body slightly, and, when you're ready, slowly open your eyes.

Now, if you're in a creative feedback group with an artist whose work you're responding to, you're ready to give feedback. Stay with your feelings. Leave your analysis for a critical audience. Criticism is also important, but it's a separate process. Try to convey to the artist everything that you experienced during the creative feedback process.

It's easiest to learn the instructions for creative feedback using a visual medium, but once you are familiar with the process, you can adapt it to other art forms. For a short piece of writing, the "flash look" might be the word or two that catches your eye in that first impression. Then you can listen to or read the poem as a whole piece. Next, read the poem more thoroughly, line by line, allowing yourself to move into and experience each image or line, and how it feels to move through it. Then choose one phrase or line to move into and become that one phrase. Going beyond what is actually written on the page, do you feel you can move outside the poem? Does it continue in a similar way or radically change?

For a longer piece of writing, or a performance piece of dance or music, the "flash look" is simply your first impression, the change from the quiet before the piece begins to the initial movement. Stay aware of your visceral experience throughout. Allow yourself to be moved by the piece; move through it, in it. Allow yourself to become the music, words, or dance, noticing the sensations in your body. When the piece ends, close your eyes and sit quietly. Be aware of any residual impressions and feelings, and intensify them. Then consciously and deliberately let them go and return to your center and the sounds in the room. Then open your eyes.

The instructions for doing creative feedback with a visual image are presented in a way that will allow you to experience the image from different perspectives, not just what is comfortable or familiar to you. For other media, the same principles of awareness apply, but the process can't be as structured. You need to open yourself to the movement of the piece as it is presented, allowing it to unfold without comments or criticism.

This kind of creative feedback requires a very deliberate commitment to stay with the direct experience, to not move away into daydreaming, numbness, or inattention. Some parts of the piece may be difficult to feel, others pleasurable, but don't try to prolong a particular feeling or hold yourself back.

It is also possible to give nonverbal feedback using touch, movement, theater, or mime. Be creative. The point is to communicate as clearly as possible your experience to the artist. One of the most pow-

erful responses that I ever received came from a performance artist. His short performance directly transmitted his experience of my photograph. When he finished, I had no doubt about what my photograph communicated to him.

Please keep in mind that in this process, your art and audience are functioning as a teacher, a guru—a mirror reflecting you back to yourself.

If you still don't understand.
Look at September, look at October.
Leaves of red and gold
Fill the valley stream.
JOHN DAIDO LOORI

※
※
※

SEVEN

Barriers

The Great Way is gateless
There are a thousand roads to it.
If you can pass through this barrier,
You will walk freely throughout the universe.

FROM WUMEN'S PREFACE TO
THE GATELESS BARRIER

As our work with the creative process evolves and we see how creativity extends beyond art into our lives, we may notice barriers that keep us from seeing in a way that's unhindered by ideas or attitudes. These barriers pop up as we struggle to find equanimity in our art and day-to-day activities.

It is critical that we acknowledge these barriers, and work through them. To be willing to find our own freedom, blocked though it may be, is the first breath of that freedom. We have to be willing to turn toward the barrier and be intimate with it. As long as we think we can run away from it or deny it, the barrier stays with us.

The following examples illustrate what I mean by barriers and how they affect our creativity and who we think we are. Sometimes the barrier takes the form of holding on to an idea such as being "original."

My good friend, Kaz Tanahashi, a Japanese calligrapher, painter, and translator, taught a workshop at Zen Mountain Monastery in 1990 called "Original Line." During the course of the workshop, he gave the participants a seemingly simple assignment: Draw a single straight line on a blank piece of paper. Not one of them did what Kaz asked.

"It was surprising," he told me later. "They drew dots, snaking lines, arches, circles. Even a spiral! Out of fourteen people, there wasn't one who stuck to the instruction. I could see their resistance to doing what I asked. A group of Japanese men and women would not have had any problem. They would have painstakingly produced a series of straight lines that looked precisely like each other. Americans are very afraid of looking alike."

A group of Japanese students might have had a different kind of barrier. But for us, the idea of originality often becomes its own prison, another way of tying ourselves up. It acts as a self-created tether. Nobody puts it around our neck but us, and we are the only ones who can take it off.

When originality becomes a goal, it is no longer original. The artist is merely trying to be different. The word "original" comes from origin, the source. Different just means something that is set apart from everything else. In the Zen arts, originality can be reached only through a long, arduous process of self-discipline and mastery of the medium. Then, ultimately, our own uniqueness naturally finds its expression.

A fundamental aspect of training in Taoist painting that was incorporated into the Zen arts was repetitive practice. The Taoist *Mustard Seed Garden Manual of Painting* is divided into several books, each with a specific subject: The Book of Trees; The Book of Rocks; of People and Things; of Orchids; Bamboo; Plum; Chrysanthemum; Grasses, Insects and Flowering Plants; Feathers and Fur; and Flowering Plants.

Students of the brush are expected to repeatedly practice the exercises in each of these books, until they can perform them fluidly and unself-consciously. For example, in the Book of Bamboo, the brushstrokes for painting the stems of bamboo are delineated first, then knots, branches, branches growing from a pair of stems, bamboo leaves, the tops of bamboo plants, horizontal branches of young bamboo, bamboo in an environment with moss, grass, water, and rocks, and bamboo shoots. Out of this repetitive practice of the strokes, students develop skill, freedom, and trust in themselves, and without any conscious effort on their part, their own uniqueness or originality begins to appear.

I am always doing that which I cannot do,
in order that I may learn how to do it.

PABLO PICASSO

Wang Anjie, the author and compiler of the *Mustard Seed Garden Manual,* said:

> First you must work hard. Bury the brush again and again in the ink and grind the ink stone to dust. Take ten days to paint a stream and five to paint a rock. Eventually you may try to paint the landscape at Jialing. Li Sixun took months to paint it. Wu Daozi did it in one evening. Thus at a later stage one may proceed slowly or carefully, or one may rely on dexterity . . . If you aim to dispense with method, learn method. If you aim at facility, work hard. If you aim for simplicity, master complexity.

This training is no different from that of the great artists of the West. Pablo Picasso's earlier works clearly reflected the discipline and training he received under the tutelage of his father—an art teacher—as well as the academies of art in which he trained. It wasn't until later in life that his own uniqueness and originality began to manifest. Originality is born of craftsmanship, skill, and diligent practice, not from trying to stand out in a crowd.

When we study with a powerful teacher, our work may begin

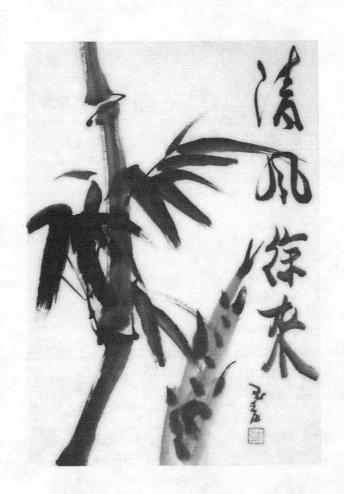

to look like the teacher's work. We lose our own identity. I had to work with this barrier when my photography started to imitate Minor's work. Minor never tried to tell us how to see. His intent in teaching photography was to free his students so that they could find their own way of expressing themselves. In my enthusiasm to "get it," I fell into a rut, trying to be someone other than who I really was. As a result, my photographs began to look more and more like Minor's.

To clear myself of Minor's way of seeing, I had to take up the barrier consciously, so I deliberately tried to imitate him. I began with a couple of his photographs, replicating their composition and tonality, as well as the feelings they conveyed. I repeated this process again and again and found that it helped me to see where and how I was being influenced. This awareness eventually led me to work from my own perspective, finding my own way of seeing and photographing.

Sometimes barriers come up when we know too much, or too little. There's a classic Zen story of a student going to visit a master artist with whom he hopes to study. The student is filled with questions, but he's also eager to make a good impression. As master and disciple sit down to talk, the young man launches into a running commentary of his opinions and ideas, obviously trying to show off his knowledge, sensitivity, and precocious skill. The master says little. He mostly listens and occasionally nods. "How about a cup of tea?" the master finally asks. He gets up and begins to prepare a pot of tea, carefully setting out a set of cups. While he's doing this, the student continues to chatter away. The master measures the leaves into the pot and pours the steaming water. As the tea brews, the student talks on about the tradition of tea, and the best place to get the finest leaves. The master begins serving, filling the student's cup to its brim. Then he continues to pour and pour, overfilling the cup, so that tea runs over the brim, to the low table, and spills on the floor. Upset, a little angry, the student wipes the table. "What are you doing?" he cries. "Can't you see the cup is full?" The master nods and smiles. "How am I to teach you anything when your cup is so full?"

Those who know don't talk.
Those who talk don't know.

LAOZI

Konstantin Stanislavsky once said, "Love the art in yourself, not yourself in the art." This is not easy for many artists, especially performers who receive a lot of attention. When we're full of ourselves, art cannot flow through us. Our art becomes rigid, limited by the boundaries we've created for ourselves, or stunted by our feelings and ideas.

Soon after we established the Zen Arts Center in 1980, I invited Watazumi Doso for an extended stay as a master in residence. Doso was a barrel-chested man, then in his late seventies, in outstanding physical condition. His huge chest was the result of years of playing bamboo flutes that ranged in length from one to eight feet. Doso, a master in the Fuke lineage of Zen, was esteemed as a Japanese national treasure. He was known for his practice of sitting under an icy waterfall near his temple while he played the flute in response to the sound of the falling water.

The bamboo flute came to Japan from China and was taken up by the Fuke monks, called "priests of nothingness." In this tradition, the flute is a special meditation tool intended to help practitioners to see their true nature and to transform their way of creating music. They would walk through the streets with bamboo baskets covering their heads, trying to play the one note that would enlighten the whole world.

If these black sleeves
Of my priestly robe
Were ample enough,
Oh, how I would envelop
All the people in need!

RYOKAN

I knew that even though Doso didn't speak a word of English, he would find a way to get his teaching across. One weekend, a rather puffed-up philosophy professor, a long-time bamboo flute aficionado, arrived to study with him. The professor brought out a very expensive and highly polished bamboo flute. Dramatically bowing to Doso, he said a little too loudly, "Please teach me." The translator relayed the message. Doso grumbled something in Japanese. The translator responded in Japanese to Doso. Back and forth they went several times until Doso's voice became gruff and demanding. The translator then turned to the professor and said, "The master said he will teach you. . . . 'Take the bamboo flute and hit yourself on the head with it.'" Before the professor had an opportunity to react, Doso began talking again. The translator continued, "The master says, if you don't want to hit yourself on the head, hand the flute over to him and he'll do it for you."

. . .

A particularly challenging barrier can often be the attachment to our creations. If we are overinvested in our art, we lose our sense of judgment. When selecting the work we would like to show an audience, we may be tempted to leave in a piece with no merit other than the pains we went through to create it.

At my early photography exhibits, I had difficulty dealing with people who didn't seem to give the photographs the time they deserved to really be seen. I had an attitude. I saw self-absorbed art "connoisseurs," strolling through the gallery, barely glancing at the photographs, yet telling me how much they enjoyed them.

Once I got so upset that I refused to sell a photograph to a man whom I felt didn't appreciate it. The owner of the gallery, understandably, pushed me to sell, so I bought the photograph myself, just to keep it out of the man's hands.

What saved me from perpetuating this torture was eventually realizing that it was painful to be so attached to my photographs. I began spending each night before an exhibition just being with the photographs, sitting quietly with them. I thanked them for the teachings I received in the process of creating them, and let them go with a bow. This helped me to shift from feeling like their creator into simply being their temporary custodian.

I said before that in order to work with a barrier you have to become intimate with it. But what happens when you're not aware of the barrier in the first place? How can you deal with it? This is where creative feedback is invaluable. It can show you your sticking places and blind spots. It's hard to go through this process alone, without a teacher or someone to provide insight into your art. That's like the eye trying to see itself.

During one of my photography outings to the Delaware River I found a beautiful spot by a waterfall flanked by some unusual rock formations. I was completely alone and feeling a deep sense of peace with myself and the environment. I was delighted to have found these rocks, convinced that there was something special to be seen and learned from them. I became absorbed in setting up my equipment and shooting, until the sound of people laughing reached my ears. At first I tried to ignore it, but curiosity finally got the better of me, and I walked upstream to find the laughter's source.

I climbed a small hill of boulders. On the other side, a group of young men and women were skinny-dipping. I watched them frolic, splashing and pushing each other playfully; then I went back to work and didn't think of them again.

After returning to my darkroom, I developed the photographs and made a set of working prints that pleased me. Later that evening, I asked my photography students if they were willing to give me some creative feedback on these photographs. "Oh, these rocks are so sensuous," one woman said. "They're so tactile and delicious," someone else said. "Very sexy." *What on earth are they talking about?!* I thought. *Are they blind to the photographs' spiritual dimensions?* I kept getting the same responses. And though at first I didn't agree with them, I had learned to trust the feedback. It was a shock to realize that while I photographed I wasn't as empty as I had thought. The experience of seeing the skinny-dippers had slipped into my subconscious, and therefore into the images I was producing.

It is true of every art that you cannot acquire what you have not felt.

GUSTIE HERRIGEL

As a result of this feedback, it became clear that my ideas regarding sensuality and spirituality were a bit confused. This became

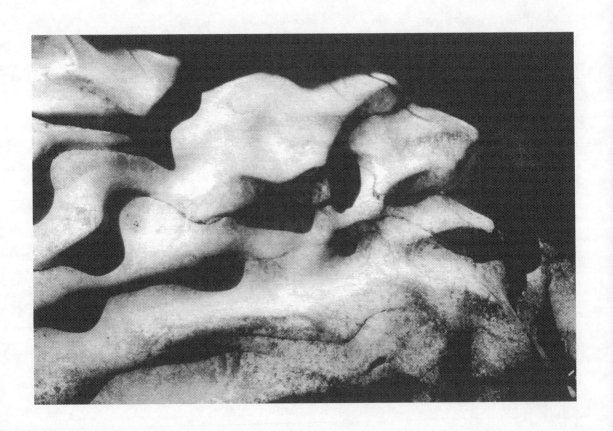

a visual koan for me. I set out deliberately to create sensual abstract images using inanimate subjects. I continued until the audience's feedback was consistent with my own feelings. It was through this process that I was able to get in touch with the feelings that were hovering in the back of my mind while I photographed.

On another occasion I had the opportunity to work in a similar manner with a more challenging aspect of my personality. I asked a date to give me feedback on a set of photographs I had just processed. We were both dressed up and ready to go out to dinner, but I was excited about these photographs, so I asked her to take a few minutes to look at them and tell me what she thought. She opened the portfolio and started flipping through the pages. Before long she was sobbing. "Why do you always take such angry pictures?!" she cried, threw the photographs on the table, and stormed from the room. That was the end of our date. I looked at the photographs, astounded. I had no idea they were going to have that effect on her.

Later that week I showed the images to my creative feedback group and got the same response. I realized that particular day of photographing had had its share of frustrations and difficulties. A commercial assignment had been fraught with problems. When I went off to photograph for myself, I carried those feelings with me. Although I told myself that what I was seeing was dynamic and exciting, in reality it was filled with my anger. I couldn't see it, but my audience clearly felt it. This, too, became a barrier with which I needed to work. I knew that I needed to get clear on anger. I needed to photograph it deliberately and feel it and see it in my photographs if I was ever going to be able to empower myself to let it go.

Barriers in the creative process sometimes appear in reaction to painful experiences, and these provide a very rich place to study ourselves. In one sense, the process is the same: The only way through the barrier is to *be* the barrier. But when what we're facing is really distressing, this may be the last thing we feel drawn to do.

Zen liturgy provides a model for working with this quandary in the offering of memorial poems at funeral services. The heart of the poem is an expression of the dharma, of the teachings. When the officiant recites a memorial poem, he or she acknowledges the person who has died and the feelings that are difficult to allow, as well as the teachings embodied in the person's life and death.

When my good friend, the poet Allen Ginsberg, died, I offered the following poem at his memorial service:

Iridescent words still dust the countryside
following the endless spring breeze like pollen
seeding mountains and rivers alike.
The bag of skin is here
but where is the bard to be found?
Aie e e e e e e e e!
Shake oh grave
the sound of the raging river
is thy howling voice.
Unborn,
unextinguished
unsilenced.

Once, years ago, following a workshop I was teaching on mindful photography, I had to work with strong residual feelings that haunted me. A magazine writer had shown up with his seventeen-year-old son to do an article on the workshop that I was leading. They hovered around, but then became interested in the workshop and decided to participate. I gave everyone an assignment, and they all went out to photograph in the rain. About an hour later, one of the participants ran back to the house in a panic. The boy had fallen out of a tree, crashing headfirst onto a stone wall below.

When I got to the boy, he was dying. Blood dripped from his ears, and I assumed that his skull was fractured. I couldn't find a pulse, and he didn't seem to be breathing. An ambulance was already on its way, but we were out in the country, and I knew it would take at least half an hour for them to get there. I began giving the boy CPR while his father stood behind me, wailing.

The boy was about the same age as my son, so I could really identify with the father. I cried as I pushed on the boy's chest, trying to blow air into him. Within a few minutes, I knew he was dead. I couldn't feel a heartbeat. Yet the father kept crying, "Save him! Save him!" so I worked on the boy until the ambulance came and I could finally step away.

I felt exhausted, but I tried to console the father and finished the workshop as best I could. Everyone was traumatized, so I worked with the participants, trying to help them process and release what had happened, but, because of my teacher's role, I couldn't do the same thing myself. In order to respond to the father and my students, I closed myself off from what I was feeling.

After the workshop, I began to have nightmares of a broken head and a gaping mouth. Then it started happening while I was awake, too. I tried everything but couldn't shake it. I sat with the feelings that the boy's death had brought up for me—the helplessness and frustration. I tried to photograph all this pent-up emotion, but a part of me resisted really confronting it. This went on for almost a year, until one day I had a deep sense that I needed to go to Cape Cod to photograph. I drove to the Cape, still carrying the image of the dead boy with me.

I spent the week sitting zazen on the beach and photographing in the area. One morning, as I was doing zazen, some kind of dead sea creature that had the size and appearance of a head washed ashore and came to rest at my feet. It was perfectly round with a gaping mouth. I went right up to it, and slowly began to photograph it. I stayed with it for several hours, and when I took the last photograph, as the shutter clicked, I could feel the release slowly moving through my body. After all that time, I was finally able to let go of the boy's death, thanks to that gift from the sea that allowed my feelings to come forth and be expressed.

Spirit always stands still long enough
for the photographer It has chosen.

MINOR WHITE

That experience taught me that working with barriers can't be rushed. We have to trust our feelings, and the natural timing of the body, even as we work toward that release through engaging the creative process. Time and patience are key.

Art koans are a unique way of addressing our barriers, making them both visible and workable through the creative process. In using koans, our intuitive aspect of consciousness must be engaged in order to reach any depth of insight into the problem we are facing.

We can actively take up our barriers as art koans. When coupled with the insight provided by the creative feedback group, the art koans become a powerful tool for moving through our barriers.

Though koans appear on the surface to be paradoxical, the fact is that there are no paradoxes. Paradox exists in language, in the words and ideas that describe the truth. Koans go beyond words and ideas to a direct and intimate experience. The answer to a koan is not a parcel of information. Rather, it's one's own intimate and direct experience of the universe and its infinite facets. In frustrating the intellect, koans dismantle the customary way of solving problems and open up new dimensions of human consciousness.

The teacher-student relationship is pivotal in traditional koan study. The teacher is not only a source for checking one's understanding, but he or she also provides invaluable guidance as the

process of resolving the koan evolves—not by explanations on how to see it, but rather through skillful, direct pointing.

From the power of
jumping into the water—
the frog can float.

TOREI ENJI

In working with art koans, the teacher is replaced by the creative feedback group. If we are able to really hear what the group is saying, we will find a tremendous source of insight into our barriers. Art koans cannot be solved intellectually. It's important that you don't try to rationalize them. Simply be aware of the feeling you'll be asked to express. Sit with the barrier, be it. Sit with the question, not its solution.

Art Koan Practice: Express Your Barrier

All of us have barriers, ranging from inconsequential obstacles that sometimes get in our way to profound barriers that arrest our activity or development. These may take the form of fear, hesitancy, anger, and prejudice. I would suggest, for this practice, that you choose a barrier that is particularly strong and persistent, one that you can easily identify with in terms of the feelings it evokes in you.

Sit with the feeling evoked by the barrier until the presence of that feeling can be felt strongly throughout your body and mind. Center that feeling in the hara and use the feeling as a guide and resonance as a compass. Find your working space and subject, and express your barrier. But be careful of merely representing your feeling. Don't paint a thunderstorm if you're feeling angry, or a pretty flower if you're happy. Dig deep and really get in touch with your feelings. Then find a subject that evokes that same feeling in you.

Again, it's critical that when you turn your work over to the creative feedback group, you let go of both the feeling and the art, and receive the feedback as a teaching. The feedback is then used as a way of returning to the practice to take it further and deeper. With each subsequent image that you create and share with your creative feedback group, there should be a significant development of your understanding of the barrier, how it functions, how you express it, and how it may be informing your art. The process should continue until you're satisfied that you've clarified this barrier in yourself.

As we work patiently with the barriers in our life, it's also important to recognize that what we've created may be private work, rather than something to offer for publication or exhibition. While it is invaluable to have friends or teachers who can do creative feedback with you, there may be times when you recognize that what you've created has a poisonous effect. Your audience may feel depleted after viewing your photographs or paintings, or reading your piece of writing. That may not be what you want to offer. Some images are poisonous and others are nourishing. When you walk away from nourishing art you feel richer, made larger than you were before approaching it. This is not an argument for "feel-good" art. But it's important to bring your attention to the effect that your art may have on your audience.

Art Koan Practice: Making Love with Light

Make love with light. Create a visual or word image of the feeling of love you have for some person, place, or thing. This means expressing the feeling itself, not simply a subject that you love.

The point of this practice is to use light in such a way that it expresses your experience of love. Find a subject that resonates with the feeling of love that you're experiencing—a subject that by virtue of its form, tones, color, shape, or context will evoke the feeling of love in your audience.

Many of our notions regarding love have been defined by our culture and our society. But what is love, really? What is love when the object of your love is not present? Is the feeling happening inside of you, or someplace else? Is love the same as possession, control, sexual fulfillment, respect, admiration? Is it joyful, hateful, blissful? Is love for a parent, a child, a lover, a pet, or your home, the same or different? Remember that this practice is not about creating a greeting card expression of love, but your own personal, direct experience.

Work with these questions as you engage the koan. Use light to communicate the feeling of love. When the process is complete, thank your subject and let it go. Present your work to your creative feedback group, using their comments to help you understand what you're communicating. Wait a few days and repeat this art koan practice until you are able to clearly express your feeling of love.

What we have been dealing with here is the tip of the iceberg. The same process can be applied to fear, anxiety, anger, creative blocks, tensions in relationships, pain—anything that stands as an obstacle in your life. Learn how to formulate it as an art koan and go to work on it.

PART III

The Artless Arts

Who calls my poems poetry?
My poems are not poetry.
Knowing that they are not poetry,
Let's start by talking together about poetry.

RYOKAN

EIGHT

The Zen Aesthetic

Up to this point we have been working with a series of ancient and modern practices and teachings that function in the arts of Zen. They inform and are reflected in a particular aesthetic unique to Zen. Over time, different art historians and commentators have attempted to define this aesthetic and its relationship to its roots in Zen Buddhism.

We have seen in working with zazen that as the meditation process deepens, a particular kind of chi or energy develops which ultimately leads to a state called samadhi, the falling away of body and mind. When this energy develops, absolute samadhi becomes working samadhi, which functions in activity. This is known as the functioning of "no mind," one of the characteristics of the Zen aesthetic.

In no mind there is no intent. The activity, whatever it may be, is not forced or strained. The art just slips through the intellectual filters, without conscious effort and without planning. This functioning of no mind is sometimes called the action of no action. This is the Taoist concept of wu-wei: a continuous stream of spontaneity that emerges from the rhythm of circumstances.

There is a clear sense of the presence of this quality in Zen paintings and poetry. It is an essential component of the martial arts. In the instant in which there is intent there is expectation. Expectation is deadly because it disconnects us from reality. When we get ahead of ourselves, we leave the moment. No mind is living in the moment, without preoccupation or projection. On the other hand, hesitancy or deliberation will show in our art when we leave the moment. Words in a poem will not flow. Notes from the flute will lack smoothness. The flower arrangement will be contrived rather than a natural reflection of nature herself.

The Zen circle of enlightenment painted by the monk Torei Enji (1720–1792) embodies the quality of no mind. Torei was one of Hakuin's chief disciples. His Zen circle is crude and closed, without the characteristic gap that Zen circles usually have. It is uneven, thick in some places, narrow in others, but bold and captivating. There is no sense that it is forced or strained. There is a feeling of emptiness and, simultaneously, of fullness and infinity. The poem included with the painting says, "In heaven and earth, I alone am the honored one." These are the words attributed to the Buddha at the time of his birth. They are an expression of the realization of his unity with the totality of the universe, where there is no subject or object, no self, no other—where the moment fills all space and time. This is no mind.

This "no mind" approach to the creation of art ultimately led to a body of work that was devoid of the usual characteristics found in sacred arts, such as perfection, grace, formality, or holiness. The sacred arts of Zen do not aspire to these ideals, but are instead imperfect and worldly. It is *through* their ordinariness that they go beyond perfection and holiness.

The great Zen master Linji said, "Followers of the way, if you want to get the kind of understanding that accords with the teachings, never be misled by others. Whether you are facing inward or facing outward, whatever you meet up with, just kill it. If you meet a buddha, kill the buddha."

The word "kill" here is not literal. It means to put an end to, or to cause to stop. That is, not to be controlled by convention, precedent, or rules, but to express one's creative energy freely and spontaneously.

When seen in paintings, this quality appears as irregularity, crookedness, unevenness, or it may be seen as the shocking or unusual turning of a phrase in a poem. Sometimes called "the rule of no rule," this characteristic reflects a fundamental aspect of Zen teachings which is called "teaching outside of patterns" or "action outside of patterns."

Zen teaching and practice tends to be expressed very directly, without excessive ornamentation. The design of a typical Zen monastery reflects this. The space is sparse, unobtrusive, and uncluttered. We see this in the simple flower arrangement on the Buddhist altar, in the architecture of the monastery's buildings, in its gardens and pathways. We also see it in the kind of food that is served and the way it is served, as well as in the practitioners' vestments. All of it reflects a simplicity that allows our attention to be drawn to that which is essential, stripping away the extra.

We hear this simplicity in the chanting during liturgy. Chants are monochromatic and follow the deep drone of a wooden drum. They tend to ground us, rather than lift us to higher states of consciousness, the way that Gregorian chants might do. The chanting has the sound of a heartbeat or the pounding of the surf.

This quality of simplicity or lack of complexity opens up a creative space that is filled with possibility. In simplicity there is a touch of boundlessness. Nothing limiting, like a cloudless sky. There is a dynamic that exists in the relationship of form to space, or of sound to silence. The moment the brush touches the blank canvas, the empty space springs into activity and enters a dynamic relationship with form. When the wooden block is struck to call practitioners to the meditation hall, the sounds are interspersed with silence of decreasing length.

This quality of simplicity is also experienced in the execution of a work of art. Calligraphy is often produced in a single stroke. Some zenga paintings are created, and haiku is recited, in a single breath:

Garden butterfly—
a child crawls to it; it flies.
He crawls; it flies.
ISSA

Our lifestyles have become extremely complex. How can we simplify our lives, reduce consumption, lower our impact on the environment, do less harm to other living things, reduce expenses, have fewer distractions, have less maintenance, enjoy more freedom and flexibility, and be able to live in a way that is financially less demanding? These are the questions that the simplicity of Zen can help to address.

Another trait of the Zen aesthetic is "no rank." Master Linji, instructing his assembly, said, "In your lump of red flesh is a true person without rank who is always going in and out of your senses. Those who have not yet realized this should look! Look!"

The true person of no rank cannot be measured or gauged. There is a sense of being matured, seasoned, or ripe. Inexperience and immaturity have vanished. In their place appears a hardiness that comes with aging.

This quality is regarded as an important element in the Zen concept of beauty, which first emerged in the Heian period when the Japanese aesthetic of poetry was being defined. No rank, or ordinariness, reflects a seasoning wherein all weakness and frailty have been removed. Sensuousness disappears and in its place surfaces a poverty in which there is nothing superfluous.

The late thirteenth-century Chinese painter Muchi's bird on an old pine is a manifestation of the quality of mystery in the Zen aesthetic. With a few bold brushstrokes, Muchi has created a timeless image. The crow is clearly the nucleus of the painting. The surrounding space gives the image openness and freedom. It clearly conveys a sense of containing within itself the totality of being. The tiny dot of the crow's eye pulls you into the painting's boundlessness.

> Deep in this mountain
> is an old pond.
> Deep or shallow,
> its bottom has never been seen.
> JOHN DAIDO LOORI

Whether we're speaking of art, religion, or life, there are always apparent edges beyond which we cannot see. As Master Dogen says, the limits of the knowable are unknowable. The process remains open. There is an element of trust that must be functioning, a trust that when the foot is thrust forward to take the next step, it will find solid ground. There is always a little bit further than can be seen.

In the Zen arts, this is reflected as implication rather than naked exposure of the whole. From within that sense of bottomlessness is born a sense of possibility and discovery. That is the way life is. That is the way truth is. It cannot be contained. It extends indefinitely and infinitely. New perspectives previously unseen appear and open up. Where does it end? It's endless. It is without boundaries. That's what makes the unknowable so wonderful and pregnant with possibilities.

Yamaoka Tesshu's (1836–1888) dragon is an embodiment of this quality. The dragon is a mysterious enlightened being in Zen lore.

Tesshu's poem accompanying the calligraphy reads: "Dragon—it feasts on sunlight and the four seas."

Despite its obvious profundity, the Zen aesthetic also contains a certain playfulness in the way the teachings are presented, perceived, and transmitted. Zen embodies a wide and unusual range of teaching methods, unique religious expressions, and a healthy ladleful of laughter, humor, clowning, and playfulness. Zen has always taken the liberty of poking fun at itself and dispelling the legend of grim austerity that people sometimes conjure up when they think of Zen because of the intensive meditation that accompanies it.

By faithful study of the nobler arts, our nature's
softened, and more gentle grows.

OVID

In the paintings of Zen we see again and again the monk Hotei, who traveled about carrying a bag of things discarded by people to give as gifts to the children he encountered along the way. He is often portrayed laughing at falling leaves and delighting in all things. During his life, people weren't sure whether he was a sage or a madman.

Master Nanquan said to Master Huangbo, "Elder, your physical size is not large, but isn't your straw hat too small?" Huangbo said, "Although that's true, still, the entire universe is within it."

ANDREW FERGUSON, TRANS., *ZEN'S CHINESE HERITAGE*

The characteristics we have been dealing with up to this point are essentially palpable qualities. Still point, no mind, simplicity, ordinariness, mystery, playfulness are traits that can be seen in a picture, heard in a poem, or perceived in a subject. There is, however, one other aspect of the Zen arts that is less obvious. We must rely on our intuitive faculties to become aware of it. It is suchness.

Suchness, or thusness, is used in Zen literature to suggest the ineffable: a truth, reality, or experience that is impossible to express in words. It refers to the "that," "what," or "it" that is self-evident and does not need explanation. It is essentially being as it is, the all-inclusive reality that is manifested as a sense of presence.

Everything should be as simple as it is,
but not simpler.

ALBERT EINSTEIN

When Yantou came to Deshan, he straddled the threshold
And asked, "Is this common or holy?"
Deshan immediately shouted.
Yantou bowed low.

BOOK OF EQUANIMITY, CASE 22, INTERNAL TRANSLATION

Thusness is the points of two arrows meeting in midair. It is a quality of being that is nondual and does not fall into either side.

Once a monastic bid farewell to Zhaozhou. Zhaozhou said, "Where are you going?"
The monastic said, "I will visit various places to study the teachings."

Zhaozhou held up the whisk and said, "Do not abide in the place where there is a buddha. Pass by quickly the place where there is no buddha. Upon meeting someone three thousand miles away, do not misguide that person."

EIHEI DOGEN'S THREE HUNDRED KOAN SHOBOGENZO, CASE 80, JOHN DAIDO LOORI AND KAZUSKI TANAHASHI, TRANS.

This holding up of the whisk points to the meeting place where differences merge.

The quality of suchness is not limited to this nondual instant of merging alone. There is more to it than that. Zen Master Yuanwu addressed the assembly, "If you want to attain the matter of suchness, you must be a person of suchness. Since you already are a person of suchness, why raise concern about the matter of suchness?"

In the words of Zen Master Dogen, "Because [the truth] is suchness, it is something that arouses the Bodhi mind spontaneously. Once this mind arises, we throw away what we played with before and we vow to hear what has not yet been heard, and we seek to verify what has not yet been verified. It is not at all our own doing."

Suchness is not something added from outside. It is being itself. It is in living life itself. It is the "isness" of a thing, indeed, the isness of existence itself. Suchness is a translation of the Sanskrit word *tatha,* sometimes used as part of the term used to refer to the Buddha: *Tathagata,* the "One Who Thus Comes." It is expressed in the calligraphy *Thus!* of Maezumi Roshi. It can be felt in Muchi's "Persimmons," six simple fruits, no two alike, suspended in space, and with an irrefutable sense of presence: Here we are!

To bring that sense of thusness into a painting, poem, or piece of music gives it a vitality that is easily experienced, although difficult to pinpoint. It may be only an instant in time, a moment out of the constant flow of life. But to sense thusness and to be able to express it brings it into our own reality.

Dirt on the cool melon
muddied
by the morning dew.
BASHO

Several hundred years later, Joyce Carol Oates expressed thusness with a similar subject in her poem "That":

A single pear in its ripeness this morning swollen ripe,
its texture rough rouged,
more demanding upon the eye than the tree
branching about it.
More demanding than the ornate grouping limbs
of a hundred perfect trees.
Yet flawed, marked as with a fingernail,
a bird's jabbing beak, the bruise of rot,
benign as a birth mark, a family blemish.
Still, its solitary stubborn weight, is a bugle,
a summoning of brass.
The pride of it subdues the orchard.
More astonishing than acres of trees, the army of ladders,
the worker's stray shouts.
That first pear's weight exceeds the season's tonnage,
costly beyond estimation,
a prize, a riddle, a feast.

As we begin to realize how to recognize suchness and move
with it, rather than opposing it, we enter a realm of harmony with
the flow of things and we're able to discover for ourselves the words
of Master Jianzhi Sengcan:

Obey the nature of things [your own nature]
and you will walk freely and undisturbed.

When thought is in bondage, the truth is hidden,
for everything is murky and unclear,
and the burdensome practice of judging
brings annoyance and weariness.
What benefit can be derived
from distinctions and separations? . . .

. . . For the unified mind in accord with the Way
all self-centered striving ceases.
Doubts and irresolutions vanish
and life in true faith is possible.
With a single stroke we are free from bondage;
nothing clings to us and we hold to nothing.
All is empty, clear, self-illuminating,
with no exertion of the mind's power.
Here thought, feeling, knowledge and imagination
are of no value.
In this world of Suchness,
there is neither self nor other-than-self.

In an attempt to deepen our appreciation of some of the characteristics we have discussed in this chapter, I would like to show how they function within some of the various Zen arts, so that we may gain insight into how they might appear in contemporary art and life.

NINE

Have a Cup of Tea

Zhaozhou questioned two new arrivals at his temple.

He asked the first monk, "Have you been here before?"

The monk said, "No, I haven't."

Zhaozhou said, "Have a cup of tea."

Then he asked the second monk, "Have you been here before?"

The monk said, "Yes, I have."

Zhaozhou said, "Have a cup of tea."

The head monk asked, "Setting aside the fact that you told the one who'd never been here before to have a cup of tea, why did you tell the one who had been here before the same thing?"

Zhaozhou said, "Head monk!"

The head monk responded, "Yes?"

Zhaozhou said, "Have a cup of tea."

EIHEI DOGEN, *THREE HUNDRED*
KOAN SHOBOGENZO, CASE 233

Tea is to East Asian Buddhism what wine is to the Judeo-Christian traditions. It holds a sacred place.

Chado, the way of tea, has been called the expression of Buddhism's spiritual, philosophical, moral, artistic, and social aspects. It embodies the spirit of the artless arts of Zen and contains all the essential characteristics that define the Zen aesthetic. Many of the other Zen arts—calligraphy, poetry, flower arrangement, and gardening—are also prominently featured in the context of the tea ceremony.

Although I've experienced the formal tea ceremony many times and in a variety of circumstances, my first encounter with it in a traditional teahouse at a small temple in Japan was a memorable occasion.

The path to the teahouse was a winding trail of stepping-stones that guided us through the tea garden. The slow approach made my companion and me appreciate the mountain setting and gently disconnected us from the urban turmoil we were leaving behind. The garden was simple, yet beautiful. Little clusters of moss on stone and a meandering stream that disappeared behind the teahouse embodied serenity and a timeless beauty.

The teahouse itself was surprising in its simplicity, contrasting

with the more elaborate buildings of the temple compound. It was a small hut, like a hermitage for a single person. It had a thatched roof and was constructed with rustic materials. The natural tones matched its setting. We approached a low stone basin into which water flowed through a bamboo pipe. We stopped to rinse our hands and mouths in a symbolic act of purification—a preparation for the ceremony.

The entryway to the hut was a four-foot-high sliding door. In order to come in, we had to lower ourselves nearly to the ground. Once inside, the first thing we encountered was the *tokonoma,* a small alcove that held a single scroll of calligraphy with a poem that was appropriate to the season. There was also a modest flower arrangement, the blossoms reflecting the spring months. The light, filtering through *shoji* screens, was subdued. The room had a soft glow to it, and the walls were bathed in gentle, warm colors. As my tea partner and I took our places, settling ourselves comfortably on the tatami mats, we could hear the sound of boiling water in a cast iron kettle and birdsong outside.

The great earth innocently
nurtures the flowers of spring.
Birds trust freely
the strength of the wind.
All this derives from the power of giving,
as does our self, coming into being.

JOHN DAIDO LOORI

Usually, conversation in a teahouse avoids business matters or controversial subjects such as politics. It focuses rather on nature and the unfolding season, or relaxed silence is maintained. In this case, we chose to simply remain silent and absorb the atmosphere.

The tea master appeared. Kneeling, he placed his fan in front of him and lowered his head to the ground, welcoming us. We returned his bow. He exited the room and began to bring in the implements for the ceremony. Holding one corner of a silk cloth in his left hand, he ran his right hand down the cloth and smoothly folded the cloth into three parts. Reaching the end of the cloth, he joined the corners together, folding the cloth again in three parts. He then used this piece of silk to symbolically clean each of the ceremonial objects—symbolically, because the tea implements were already meticulously clean. He ritualistically rinsed the bowls with hot water taken from the kettle as we watched. He dipped a bamboo whisk in the water, examined it, and placed it to one side. He poured the hot water into the tea bowl, and then wiped the bowl with a damp cloth.

The master gestured to us, inviting us to enjoy the sweets that he had placed before us. While we ate, he proceeded to prepare the tea. With deft movements he opened the tea caddy and with a bent bamboo spoon measured jade green powdered tea into the bowl. He dipped a long-handled dipper into the kettle and poured hot water onto the tea. Then, with a bamboo whisk, he whisked the tea into a froth. He turned and set a bowl in front of me, with the most striking side of the bowl deliberately facing toward me. I lifted the bowl and brought it closer. I bowed to my tea partner. I lifted the bowl into the palm of my hand and turned it two short turns so its "front" faced away from me. I bowed to the tea and drank it in a few sips, slurping the last bit, which is considered in good taste in Japan.

Finishing the tea, I rotated the bowl to its original position and placed it on the floor in front of me. I bowed. The tea master retrieved the bowl and washed it with hot water. Meanwhile, my companion enjoyed his tea. After he was finished and the master had cleaned his bowl, the master returned the bowls to us so we could examine them and appreciate their uniqueness.

Historically, many of the most sought-after bowls for tea ceremony in Japan were dull colored and roughly finished, not elegant or refined in their craftsmanship. A few of the favored tea bowls were originally inexpensive but wonderful Korean rice bowls intended for everyday use. They were accidental masterpieces of form and design—asymmetrical, cracked, occasionally wobbly, with a thick coating of glaze and an unglazed foot.

The appreciation of the utensils and bowls we used was an important part of the ceremony. Each of them was picked especially for us, brought out for the occasion by our host. We leisurely examined the bowls and the utensils, appreciating their finer qualities, and then returned them to the tea master. He put them away in a little alcove and returned to kneel in front of us. The ceremony concluded the way it began. He placed his fan on the ground in front of him and lowered his head to the floor. We returned the bow, and he retired to the alcove. We left the way we came, down the winding path through the garden, back into the fray of our lives, yet somehow more buoyant, more fulfilled than when we had entered the teahouse.

I realized that the tea ceremony was a manifestation of the merging of host and guest, the apparent differences that are spoken of in the teachings of Zen, as well as a beautiful reflection of the liturgy I had experienced in Zen monasteries.

A well-performed tea ceremony will provide the participants with the taste of certain qualities of the artless arts. To the eye of an experienced tea master, the tea bowls display wabi and sabi, qualities that have become synonymous with the Zen aesthetic. Wabi is a feeling of loneliness or solitude, reflecting a sense of nonattachment and appreciation for the spontaneous unfolding of circumstances. It is like the quiet that comes from a winter snowfall, where all the sounds are hushed and stillness envelops everything. Sabi is the suchness of ordinary objects, the basic, unmistakable uniqueness of a thing in and of itself.

Two other qualities used to describe the feelings that Zen art evokes are aware and yugen. Aware is a feeling of nostalgia, a longing for the past, for something old and worn. It's an acute awareness of the fleeting nature of life, its impermanence. Yugen is the mystery, the hidden, indescribable, or ineffable dimensions of reality. These qualities are expressed by the bowls, the hut, the master's movements. They are in the atmosphere itself. This is the classic expression of the Zen aesthetic, which can be found not only in the arts of Zen, but throughout Japanese culture as well.

If only you could hear
the sound of snow . . .

HAKUIN EKAKU

There is also the overarching theme of poverty in chado—not the poverty of down and out, but of bare-bones simplicity, the simplicity of not clinging to anything.

Ryokan, a Zen master and poet, lived in a simple thatched hut. He was born around 1758 and ordained at the age of eighteen. Shortly after receiving dharma transmission, Ryokan's teacher died. The poet went to live in a hermitage on Mount Kugami, where he spent his time sitting zazen, talking to visitors, and writing poetry. Many stories of Ryokan's simplicity and his love for children have come down to us, as well as of his indifference for worldly honor. In fact, Ryokan called himself Daigo (Great Fool).

One evening, when Ryokan returned to his hut, he surprised a thief who was naively trying to rob the hermit. There was nothing to steal in the hut. Yet Ryokan, feeling sorry for him, gave him his clothes, and the thief, shocked, ran away as fast as he could. Ryokan, shivering as he sat naked by the window, wrote the following haiku:

> The burglar
> neglected to take
> the window's moon.

To be simple means to make a choice about what's important, and to let go of all the rest. When we are able to do this, our vision expands, our heads clear, and we can better see the details of our lives in all their incredible wonder and beauty.

Simplicity does not come easily to us in the West. In general, we don't like to give anything up. We tend to accumulate things, thinking that if something is good, we should have more of it. We go through life hoarding objects, people, credentials, ignoring the fact that the more things we have to take care of, the more burdensome our lives become. Our challenge is to find ways to simplify our lives.

Rikyu, the founder of the tea ceremony, was a serious student of Zen. He spent many years in rigorous training in the monasteries of Japan. After perfecting the ritual aspects of the tea ceremony, he became widely known and respected. Rikyu's close friend, the shogun, regularly frequented Rikyu's teahouse. The shogun, Toyotomi Hideyoshi, though known to be a despot, was also a great patron of the tea ceremony. In praise of Rikyu he recited the following poem at one of his tea parties:

> When tea is made with water drawn from the depths of
>   Mind
> We really have what is called chado.

One summer, Rikyu managed to acquire blue morning glory seeds, virtually unknown in Japan at the time. He planted them in the garden around his tea hut. This was discussed widely, and eventually word of the morning glories reached the shogun. He sent his messenger to tell the tea master that he would come for tea in order to see the new flowers. A couple of days later, the shogun appeared at Rikyu's place, but when he strolled into the garden, he couldn't find a single morning glory.

"Where are those beautiful new flowers I've been hearing so much about?" asked the shogun.

"I had them removed," answered Rikyu.

"Removed!" said the shogun, surprised and not a little perturbed. "Why?"

"Come," said Rikyu, leading the shogun to the teahouse. The shogun angrily removed his swords and shoes and then bowed down to enter through the low door of the tea room. In the tokonoma, resting in a slim bronze vase, lay a single, freshly cut morning glory, still wet with the morning dew. At that instant, without any distractions standing in the way, the shogun saw that flower, singular in its beauty, completely filling his universe.

All beings are flowers
Blooming
In a blooming universe.

SOEN NAKAGAWA

The quality of simplicity that is present in traditional Zen monasteries also exists in Zen gardens. A Zen garden features a few carefully placed rocks, raked sand, and trees trimmed to expose the

hills in the distance. Each rock is chosen because of its characteristic shape and form. In the West, by contrast, our gardens tend to overflow with beauty, so much of it that we miss the beauty.

Our culture of excess is growing, infiltrating even our most basic activities. Overeating and obesity are epidemic in the United States. The size of servings at restaurants has doubled in the past twenty years. In Japanese restaurants a small steak comes on a very large plate with a little cluster of potatoes, a few spears of vegetables, and a sprig of parsley. The portion is reasonable in size and appealing in its presentation, with the same dynamic of form and space seen in a Zen garden. We are nourished by the presentation as we are nourished by the food. And we walk away a little hungry. My dharma grandfather Yasutani Roshi used to say, "You should always stop eating before you feel completely full." That's one of the themes in *oryoki,* the ceremonial meal taken at Zen monasteries during long meditation intensives.

In developing the tea ceremony, Rikyu was influenced by oryoki or *juhatsu,* the liturgy of eating practiced respectively in the Soto and Linji schools of Zen. *Oryoki* roughly means "that which contains just enough," and it also refers to the Buddha bowl monks receive at their ordination. Oryoki, like the tea ceremony, is a very detailed ritual. Each movement is attended to with care and painstaking detail. Everyone begins and finishes together. Starting with the five bowls that are lined up over a folded cloth, to the serving and receiving of the food, to the cleaning and wrapping of the bowls, each movement in oryoki is precise and deliberate. Chants accompany the ceremony, which emphasizes that what is taking place is not only the ordinary act of eating, but a sacred activity.

In Zen monasteries, the beginning and end of each activity is punctuated with appropriate liturgy. This ranges from a simple gesture of placing both hands palm-to-palm together in gassho and bowing before entering a room, to an elaborate, two-hour-long funeral service. This mindful engagement of an activity is designed to help us awaken to what we are about to do. Formal ceremonies, work and study, the practical functions of eating and washing are all carried out with a mind that is alert, attentive, and completely present. When the mind is in that state, every single thing we encounter is as complete and simple as Rikyu's morning glory.

It is easy to imagine that the formality of the tea ceremony or oryoki is confining, or that the spirit of simplicity calls for everything to be stripped away, leaving only a bare form. Nothing could be further from the truth. When completely embodied, the true spirit of simplicity is freedom in action. Within the specific form we become free of that form.

Once, Soen Roshi and a group of students were meeting someone at Kennedy Airport in New York City. One of the students arrived late. When he appeared, Soen said to him, "You missed the tea ceremony."

"A tea ceremony at Kennedy Airport?" said my friend, looking around him incredulously. "Where?"

"Ah," mused Soen. "Maybe you're not too late. Come with me." Soen dragged him into a nearby doorway. Two women rushed by pulling huge suitcases behind them, while a man waved frantically at someone in the distance. They didn't notice a strange Japanese man in flowing robes with his arm around his bewildered companion.

Soen reached into his sleeve and pulled out a little porcelain container with powdered green tea and a small bamboo spoon. He took a spoonful of tea and said, "Open your mouth." My friend obeyed and Soen plopped the tea in his mouth, lifted his chin so his jaw was closed, and said, "Now, make water."

The elaborate ritual of the classic tea ceremony, which can take over an hour, was reduced to its essence in this simple act. All that was left was the taste of tea.

The fact that both of these manifestations of tea ceremony—Soen's improvisational form and the traditional and elaborate ritual—can exist side by side is a testimony to the true spirit of freedom implicit in the teachings and practice of the Zen arts.

Ultimately, oryoki, like the tea ceremony, is a state of mind. It has nothing to do with a set of bowls or being in a meditation hall. It has everything to do with being completely present, and doing what we're doing while we're doing it—whether we're at a Burger King, an airport, or a monastery. If our mind is cluttered with thoughts or worries, we're not doing oryoki. We're not being simply present. The way we use our mind is the way we live our lives. If we understand these principles and take them up as practice, we will liberate ourselves.

There was an old tea master who received notice that a high official would be coming to have tea at his teahouse. He directed his young apprentice to prepare the garden for the guest. The apprentice worked diligently all morning, raking and clearing the garden of fallen leaves that had cluttered the streams and the rock gardens. He persisted until the garden was meticulously clean, not a stray leaf in sight. When he asked the tea master to examine his work, the master looked at it and said, "Almost perfect, but not quite." Then he walked over to a couple of the maple trees and shook them lightly so a few crimson leaves fell on the path and garden.

For simplicity to be simple, it needs to be natural, almost unnoticeable. It can't be contrived or forced. The meticulous garden calls attention to itself by virtue of its meticulousness. Going a bit further with this story, I would say, let the leaves just fall on the path by themselves.

Layman Pang, a ninth-century Chinese Zen master, had his own version of simplicity. Realizing that he wanted to devote the rest of his life to the spiritual path, Pang loaded all of his possessions onto a boat and sunk them in a river. I've always wondered why he didn't give his stuff away to people who could have used it. His intent was noble, but he went a bit overboard.

Being simple doesn't mean being simpleminded. It doesn't mean indiscriminately getting rid of everything you don't want, or doing away with form, style, or discipline. Nor is it the other extreme: enduring the discomforts of simplification, putting yourself through a heroic cleansing, a forced renunciation or asceticism.

Renunciation is not giving up the things of this world, but accepting that they go away.

SHUNRYU SUZUKI

Many years ago I set off on a weeklong canoe trip in the headwaters of the Oswegatchie River in upstate New York. Arthur, a Jamaican friend, who had spent most of his life hunting, fishing, and backpacking, generously offered to accompany me. I loved the outdoors, but had never spent an extended period of time cross-country camping.

Arthur arrived at Cranberry Lake village, where we had agreed to meet, just as I was cramming the last of my gear into the pack. My canoe, *Chestnut Darling,* was on the ground next to the car. Arthur took one look at my pack and burst out laughing. "Man, you got the white man syndrome!" he said, shaking his head. I stared at him blankly. "What are you trying to do—bring your entire house with all of its comforts into the woods?"

I looked at my pack. Every single compartment, down to the tiniest pocket, was filled with various items. I thought all of them were necessary. It didn't take me long to find out that trying to carry a ninety-five-pound pack across long canoe portages was not only uncomfortable, but unnecessary. I couldn't keep up with Arthur. Still shaking his head and grinning, he switched packs with me, and carried my "house" for the rest of the trip. To his credit, he agreed to go out with me again. Next time around we trimmed my pack down to sixty-five pounds.

As time went by, my love of camping grew, and my packing ability improved. First, I did away with the extras, the little amenities that were really not necessary to survive, like books. Then I stopped taking pots and silverware. I cooked food in my army surplus canteen cup and ate with my sheath knife. Seeing how much I could pare down became both a challenge and an obsession. I did away with all my extra clothes, and learned to pack just enough food to last me the length of the trip. With each successive outing, my pack got leaner and leaner, and I realized I did not miss the equipment at all. On the contrary, I felt lighter, freer, and more in touch with my surroundings than I had before.

My wife did not share my enthusiasm for minimalist camping, and since I was adamant about not bringing anything on our trips that wasn't absolutely necessary, she began to smuggle silverware and books by taping them to her body.

One late summer in 1965 I returned to the headwaters of the Oswegatchie, this time by myself. I set up camp in the early evening and the next morning packed my camera and a knapsack with a small survival kit, intending to spend the day photographing a distant mountain lake I had spotted on my map. The day was cool and overcast, the light perfect for photographing. I hiked a couple of miles to a small swamp, waded slowly through it, and continued. I made my way up the mountains until I reached the lake. It was a small but beautiful expanse of water, its slate-gray surface rippling softly in the wind.

I shot through the changing light, but before long it started to rain and I had to pack my gear. The rain turned into a downpour. I thought I could wait it out, but after a couple of hours it still hadn't let up. I decided that the best thing would be to return to my campsite. I made my way down the mountain, through the woods, and back to the swamp, only to discover that the rain had turned it into a pond that was too deep to cross. I tried to find my way around it, but couldn't. Night was falling, it was turning cold, and the storm continued in full force. I didn't think I would be able to retrace my path in the dark, so I decided to stay where I was until morning.

I felt both apprehensive and excited as I searched for high ground, far from the water in case it continued to rise. Here was a real test of my ability to make do without gear. I began by creating a small circle of rocks in front of a large boulder that would reflect the heat of a fire. I rigged my poncho into a lean-to, then built a small fire and made a cup of broth from a packet that I always carried in my survival kit. Tired, and warm from the soup, I settled down with my back against a tree.

Arm for a pillow, watching the gemlike
raindrops from the eaves, alone.

BASHO

When I awoke in the middle of the night, the storm was still sweeping over the mountains, but I was perfectly warm and dry. I threw more wood on the fire, watching the storm. I slept on and off until morning, and in the light of day it was easy to bushwhack my way around the pond and pick up the trail that led back to my camp.

That trip completely changed the way I perceived camping. I realized that with a bit more food, I could have stayed out for several days. Even the minimal pack that I was so proud of had proved unnecessary. These days, I camp with a tent, a stove, and silverware again, but I haven't lost the spirit of simplicity I touched in those early trips.

The Zen arts in their bare-bone simplicity and sobriety may sometimes appear archaic, but they are surprisingly modern, both in ap-

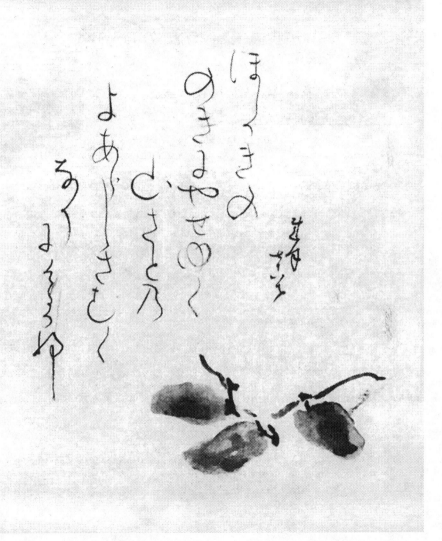

ほしこきの
のきはやをゆく
ひとかけ
よあけしゆく
るくよ

pearance and function. The lines of a classic Japanese teahouse, rock garden, or a simple ceramic pot are invariably clean and elegant. By avoiding overstatement, the Zen artist conveys the impression of disciplined restraint, of having held something in reserve. And in the art's empty spaces we sense a hidden plenitude. The result is a feeling of implied strength, a suspicion that we have only glimpsed the power and full potential of the artist.

In a society that assures us that more is better, it's not always easy to trust that we have enough, that we *are* enough. We have to cut through the illusion that abundance is security, and trust that we don't have to buffer ourselves against reality. If we have learned to trust abundance, we can learn to trust simplicity. We can practice simplicity.

Zen, and by extension the Zen aesthetic, shows us that all things are perfect and complete, just as they are. Nothing is lacking. In trying to realize our true nature, we rub against the same paradox: We don't know that we already are what we are trying to become. In Zen, we say that each one of us is already a buddha, a thoroughly enlightened being. It's the same with art. Each one of us is already an artist, whether we realize it or not. In fact, it doesn't matter whether we realize it—this truth of perfection is still there. Engaging the creative process is a way of getting in touch with this truth, and to let it function in all areas of our lives.

No creature ever comes short of its own completeness.
Wherever it stands, it does not fail
to cover the ground.

EIHEI DOGEN

If I was asked to get rid of the Zen aesthetic and just keep one quality necessary to create art, I would say it's trust. When you learn to trust yourself implicitly, you no longer need to prove something through your art. You simply allow it to come out, to be as it is. This is when creating art becomes effortless. It happens just as you grow your hair. It grows.

TEN

Dancing Brush

*Man is a thinking reed but his great works are done when
he is not calculating and thinking. "Childlikeness" has to be
restored with long years of training in the art of self-forgetfulness.
When this is attained, man thinks yet he does not think. He
thinks like the showers coming down from the sky; he thinks
like the waves rolling on the ocean; he thinks like the stars
illuminating the nightly heavens; he thinks like the green foliage
shooting forth in the relaxing spring breeze. Indeed, he is the
showers, the ocean, the stars, the foliage. When a man reaches this
stage of "spiritual" development, he is a Zen artist of life.*

D. T. SUZUKI

During the fall of 1947, I was stationed as a boatswain's mate, third class, on a navy destroyer in the Mediterranean. One night we were in a port somewhere in the Persian Gulf known for its anti-American sentiments. I was on sentry duty on deck. Because of the possibility of hostile actions, we had strict orders to use lethal action to stop unauthorized boarders. These orders were written out in a directive that each sentry carried with him.

Around three o'clock in the morning I heard a sound coming from the darkness at the stern of the ship. I moved toward the noise and saw a man climbing over the railing. I unshouldered my rifle and pointed it straight at him. "Halt!" I shouted. The man stopped briefly, looked straight at me, and just kept coming. "Halt or I'll shoot!" To frighten him, I cocked the rifle and let an unspent shell pop from the chamber onto the deck. He didn't even flinch. I cocked the rifle again, but couldn't bring myself to pull the trigger. The man walked toward me, then past me to the garbage cans standing a few feet to the side. He filled a bag with the uneaten remains of our evening meal, carried it to the railing, and lowered it to a woman who was waiting in a rowboat, holding on to our propeller guards. He slid down the rope and they rowed away, disappearing into the blackness.

I could have shot him. According to my orders, I should have. It would have been perfectly legal, but morally wrong. The man was hungry. His whole family was probably hungry. That's all. I don't know what stopped me from pulling the trigger, something deeper than my orders, something that I referred to in the chapter on the artless arts as the rule of no rule.

Zen training is very formal and disciplined. Yet, the whole point of the practices and the forms it embraces is freedom. This is the characteristic of the rule of no rule. On one hand, we have rigor, formalism, and repetition. On the other, we constantly hear the refrain "trust yourself"; don't put another head on top of your own. We practice within that dynamic tension. The freedom of Zen and the Zen arts appears not in rejection or disregard of form, but within the form itself. It unfolds as practice. It is there that it becomes the form of no form, the effort of no effort, the rule of no rule.

One has not understood until one has forgotten it.

D. T. SUZUKI

When Watazumi Doso came to visit Zen Mountain Monastery, I gave him a tour of the grounds. We came upon a plumber who was working on our new bathhouse. Cast-iron piping lay outside the building. Doso playfully picked up a three-foot-long piece and began to play it as though it was a shakuhachi flute. Although the pipe had no holes in it, he was able to create a surprisingly wide range of sounds and a haunting melody.

Doso gave a concert at the Zen Center of Los Angeles and soon after the performance started, an LAPD helicopter flew into the area and hovered overhead. TUM! TUM! TUM! TUM! Doso's flute

immediately picked up the rhythm and developed a counterpoint. An infant cried. Doso's flute responded. A car drove by at high speed. The flute whizzed with it. Doso's concert included the totality of all the sounds that were happening around us. He blended, merged, answered everything he heard, incorporating it into his experience and expression, rather than being distracted by it.

This ability to be free in his music was the result of Doso's lifelong, unrelenting commitment to the discipline of the breath. He actually wasn't very interested in the shakuhachi as a musical instrument. He called his flute *suijo,* which loosely translates as "concentrated breathing tool." Doso saw himself not so much as a musician or entertainer, but as one who is totally devoted to developing his life force—chi—by utilizing and strengthening his breath. The bamboo flute was simply a tool for that practice. He said once, "Since I must have some way of knowing how my breath is doing, I blow into a piece of bamboo and hear how it sounds."

Doso didn't use the highly polished lacquered and well-tuned flutes that were common in the Japanese shakuhachi tradition. His flute was much less processed and far closer to its natural state. The inside of the section he used still revealed the bamboo guts. Most people, even experienced masters, considered that kind of instrument unplayable. Doso's music proved that wrong. His playing always touched the very core of one's being. Sometimes the sound had a tremendous strength, like the driving force of a cascading waterfall. Sometimes it roared like thunder. At other times it was gentle and sweet like birdsong at sunrise. It always seemed to reach me, but not through my ears: It entered my body through the base of my spine, moved upward, and spread through my being.

Just like shakuhachi, *shodo,* the way of the brush, is a traditional form of the artless arts of Zen. This form encompasses the calligraphy of Zen teachings and poems, as well as the painting of images. In either case, the effectiveness of brushwork as a practice rests in the instantaneous interaction of the ink and the paper or silk. The brush must move continuously over the absorbent surface for the ink to flow smoothly. Any hesitancy, any afterthought, any anticipation, immediately shows. Brushwork requires the free movement of hand, arm, and mind. When mastered, the repertoire of brushstrokes ranges from delicate elegance to rough vitality, from minutely detailed images to massive, bold outlines. This is particularly true in the *zenga* style of painting.

Ga means painting, so zenga means Zen painting. Zenga is not really a school, but rather a term for art created by a Zen master. John Stevens, a Soto Zen monk, scholar, artist, and author writes in *Zenga: Brushstrokes of Enlightenment:*

> Zenga represents spiritually and artistically the expressive art of Zen masters who created free and personal interpretations that contrasted dramatically in style with the rigidity of the traditional Buddhist painting that existed at the time.
>
> Although permeated with humor, joy and unrestrained freedom, Zen painting and calligraphy is comprised of far more than lighthearted cartoons, witty sayings and delightful abstract images. True art always imparts a deep message as profound and universal as that revealed in the most venerable religious text, or the most challenging philosophical treatise. It is a misconception to think of Zen art as a pleasant diversion from more "serious" forms of religious and artistic expression. On the contrary, a single Zen brushstroke by an enlightened master can reveal a new reality to the viewer.

To paraphrase E. John Bullard, director of the New Orleans Museum of Art in his foreword to *Zenga: Brushstrokes of Enlightenment,*

Japanese culture has always appreciated Zen painting for its religious content, but it is only recently that Western collectors and museums have become aware of this. Critics, curators, particularly in the United States, have begun to appreciate the unique aesthetic that is present in zenga. Without an understanding of Buddhism or the Japanese language, Westerners are able to grasp the aesthetic significance of this art form.

Zenga art is asymmetrical, without regular, recognizable geometrical shapes to anchor our eye. The brush lines are usually jagged, gnarled, irregular, twisting, dashing, sweeping. Zenga is bold and immediate, and almost always created spontaneously, in a single breath.

In many cases, a zenga painting acts as a visual koan or sermon whose teaching is offered through very concise, direct pointing. This form of teaching is still employed by many Zen teachers, East and West. In my own work I employ both Chinese and Roman calligraphy, zenga, and—in the last twenty years—modern media, specifically photography and videography, as a way of communicating the teachings.

Jikihara Sensei is an eighty-year-old master of the *nanga* style of painting, a form of brushwork developed in China that includes both monochrome and color images. He is a recognized lineage holder in the Obaku school of Zen and the abbot of a small temple in Japan.

The Obaku school is one of three Zen schools, along with Rinzai and Soto, still active in Japan. Its head temple, Mampukuji, is at Uji in Kyoto. The school was named after the Chinese master Huangbo (J. Obaku) and was brought to Japan in the seventeenth century by Yinyuan Lungji. Obaku Zen took shape during the Ming dynasty in China from a mixture of Zen and Pure Land Buddhism, and through the years it developed a small following.

A nanga and a zenga painting's execution differ in that zenga paintings tend to be simple, direct. On the other hand, nanga painting evolves over a longer period of time, each brushstroke suggesting the next. New visual tensions are created as the painting develops. Although nanga embodies the basic principles of Chinese brushwork, it also has a relationship to watercolors. I have watched Jikihara produce full-color paintings in the style and aesthetic of nanga.

In the early 1980s, Jikihara was a teacher-in-residence at Zen Mountain Monastery, and I had numerous opportunities to watch him display his skill and amazing naturalness and spontaneity. These demonstrations reminded me of watching Soen do calligraphy, but the intervening years of training and study gave me a deeper appreciation of the way Jikihara's art embodied the timeless principles of Zen.

One evening, several of us gathered around as Jikihara set out to do a large painting. His wrinkled face and mane of white hair conjured a master from ancient China. He laid out several brushes, a shallow dish, a small container of water, ink stone, ink wedge, and a three-by-five-foot sheet of paper, anchored at the corners with pebbles. He began working the ink, rubbing the wet ink stone with a wedge of pressed pine resin and soot. Jikihara worked with an intense attentiveness, constantly examining the ink's density and viscosity.

When he was satisfied with the ink's quality, he began to work one of the brushes in the ink, dipping it, rotating it, pressing it along the ink stone until it had just the right amount of flexibility and the right amount of ink. He moved over the paper and tilted slightly forward, the brush poised in his right hand. He seemed suspended in space. Everyone was quiet. It felt like he was drinking in the blank sheet of paper, imagining the space filling with the image. His brush moved to a precise spot in this emptiness. A dab of ink activated it. The dance began.

As the painting unfolded, I noticed that the first spot of ink defined what would grow out of and around it. That first spot is like the seed of a pine tree. If a pine takes root on the edge of a cliff, its trunk and branches are stunted, its needles short. The same seed planted in a forest of pine trees grows narrow and tall, with branches that have a very short reach. In the middle of an empty field, the trunk is wide, the branches reaching out many feet, its shape more round than tall. The pine's growth and development always directly responds to the environment, to nutrients, soil, temperature, and weather. Likewise, the shape that follows the first mark on paper is an organic response to the touch of the brush and to its environment.

A painting evolves from the dynamic play between the painter and the circumstances. If the painter begins with preconceived notions of what the finished work should look like, her ideas will preclude the occurrence of exciting "accidents" of the brush, like the splattering of ink that gives so much of Zen painting its character and richness.

This kind of organic unfolding occurred as Jikihara's image began to appear—eyes, head, then a body. He occasionally changed brushes to get the correct tonal consistency. To get a range of tones out of one stroke, he would soak a brush in water and ink to produce a shade of gray. The tip of the brush was then dipped into pure black ink. As he moved the brush over the paper, he would guide it while pressing the heel of the brush down so the gray color would spread. At first, his movements were slow and deliberate. As the painting filled in, his brushwork became swifter. It was astonishing to watch an old man move with such energy and vitality. It was as if he was drawing chi from the art as it evolved, and then returning it to the painting in subsequent brushstrokes.

It took twenty-five minutes for Jikihara to complete his work. His last marks were slight and very precise touches of the brush. I saw that at this point the smallest stroke had the power to alter dras-

tically the piece's appearance and mood. Finally, Jikihara stepped back from the painting and took it in. He wrote a short verse on its edge and put the brush down. We applauded; he bowed.

Jikihara's painting was a classic presentation of the seventh-century Chinese hermit and poet Hanshan (J. Kanzan) and his fellow poet Shide (J. Jitoku, which literally means "the foundling"): two recluses who lived during the Tang dynasty on Cold Mountain in China.

The little we know about Hanshan was written by an official of the Tang dynasty named Lujiu Yin. There are no accurate dates for the poet's lifetime, but he was said to live sometime between the late sixth and the late ninth century.

Hanshan was a poor and eccentric scholar who lived in retirement in a mountain cave. He dressed in rags. Shide worked in the kitchen of a nearby temple and would give Hanshan bits of leftover food to take home. Hanshan's poems were gathered by Lujiu Yin from where they had been inscribed on trees, rocks, houses, and on the walls of the cave in which Hanshan lived. The collection contained over three hundred poems. Most of them are attributed to Hanshan, and a few to Shide.

In Jikihara's presentation, the two mountain hermits are reading a sheet of poetry and laughing together. They were known for their profound realization and their simple lifestyle. Throughout history, they've been a favorite subject for painters, and countless scrolls depict them. Jikihara's was one more of these paintings, yet his brushwork gave the subject a unique and completely new expression, full of mirth, lightness, and a deep feeling for life.

Soen Roshi also had an unprecedented ability to be completely free in his calligraphy, an ability that blurred the edge between art and life. While visiting the house of a friend who studied Zen with Soen, I noticed in his recreation room, hanging over the bar, a watery, red calligraphy, signed with Soen's name. I suspected that there might be a story associated with it, so I asked—and indeed, there was.

During a visit, my friend offered Soen a drink. Soen pointed to an attractive bottle of grenadine. The host tried to persuade Soen to drink something else, explaining that grenadine is not usually imbibed straight, but Soen persisted. My friend poured him a healthy shot of the red syrup in a brandy glass. As Soen lifted the glass to his lips, he realized his mistake. Without missing a beat, he placed the glass back on the bar. Rather than wasting the drink, Soen turned to my friend and asked for his brush. Then he proceeded to execute a beautiful calligraphy using the syrup as ink.

One who has attained mastery of an art
reveals it in every action.

SAMURAI MAXIM

Soen's style of teaching Zen was as liberating as his capacity with the brush. He remained true to tradition, yet never allowed it to become stale, predictable, or conventional. You had to be on your toes to study with him. You couldn't take anything for granted. He was always full of surprises.

A student of mine once did a sesshin (a silent meditation retreat) that Soen was leading in a house where the interview room for dokusan was on the second floor, a flight up from the meditation hall. When the bell rang, the next person on the dokusan line had to go up to see Soen. My student told me that when it was her turn, she got to the bottom of the stairs, looked up, and saw Soen on the second-floor landing. He waved to her urgently, saying, "Come on! Hurry! Hurry!" She raced up the stairs. When she got to the top, Soen grabbed her by the arm and ran her down the hall into a room.

He threw open the blinds and, pointing, exclaimed, "Look!" A large full moon, perfect in its roundness, was just rising above the mountain. She said she will never forget that moon. Or Soen.

In creating art, the rule of no rule, or spontaneity, refers to a process that is organic, intuitive, and uncultivated. Spontaneity is inherently human; it is wild and untaught. It is the truth that has no teacher. Nobody can give you spontaneity. Why? Because you already have it. It simply needs to be awakened and manifested. It needs to be realized and actualized. And you're the only one who can do it. You are the only one who can practice it.

> *To what shall*
> *I liken the world?*
> *Moonlight, reflected*
> *in dewdrops*
> *shaken from a crane's bill.*
>
> EIHEI DOGEN

Spontaneity relates to art in which there is no artificiality or contrivance. Art that is natural expresses the artist's direct experience of reality, the multiplicity of the universe that each one of us experiences every moment, without self-consciousness.

When I was nine years old, I studied the clarinet with a professor of music. I practiced daily until I was sixteen. When I went off to join the navy, I forgot all about it. Some forty-five years later, one of my Zen students restored a beautiful clarinet and gave it to me as a birthday gift. When I opened it, the people gathered at my birthday party immediately asked me to play. I was very excited to be holding a clarinet after so many years, so I dove right in. I played an

entire piece without missing a note. Rather, the piece played itself. Everyone applauded and egged me on to play more, but before I could begin, my brain clicked into gear. *I haven't played in years. What if I make a mistake? What if I embarrass myself?* And on and on. I tried to play and fumbled. Once my mind began moving, worrying about what I was supposed to accomplish, I froze.

Spontaneity is not reflective or calculating. It does not concern itself with the outcome. Zen master Daito Kokushi, even though he was a teacher of great renown, refused any claim to fame. He was born in 1282 into a samurai family in the country west of Tokyo. After receiving recognition as a Zen master from his teacher, Daio Kokushi, Daito went into seclusion. He wore a robe made of reeds and lived among the beggars at the Fifth Street Bridge in Kyoto.

The emperor, anxious to have Daito teach at his court, sent out a group of soldiers to ferret out the great master. Knowing that Daito loved melons, the emperor told the soldiers to offer each beggar a melon in such a way that only Daito would be able to respond. The soldiers took with them a cart full of melons, and, as each beggar approached, they said, "Take this melon without using your hands." Finally it was Daito's turn. The soldier repeated the command. Without a moment's hesitation, Daito replied, "Give it to me without using your hands."

The soldiers nabbed Daito and took him to court, where, at the emperor's request, he founded Daitokuji monastery, one of the monasteries in which Rikyu was purported, centuries later, to teach the tea ceremony.

Another characteristic of Zen arts closely related to spontaneity is playfulness. It often appears as humor or willingness to be unconventional, even irreverent. The Indian monk Bodhidharma, regarded as the founder of Zen and the equivalent of a saint in Zen Buddhism, is also referred to as the "broken-toothed old barbarian."

Chinese and Japanese Zen portraits depict him as a scraggly old guy without eyelids. Legend has it that the master ripped off his eyelids so he wouldn't fall asleep during zazen. Tea plants sprang up where his eyelids landed. That's why Zen monks traditionally drink green tea to stay awake during meditation periods. Bodhidharma is one of Zen Buddhism's most important figures, yet the only portraits we have of him are caricatures.

Master Hakuin, who was responsible for many of the more irreverent portraits of Bodhidharma, consistently injected humor into his writings, calligraphy, and paintings. His images are always surprising, sharp in their social and spiritual commentary, and although they poke fun at our foibles and the dark side of humanity, they are never poisonous. Hakuin's art reminds us not to take ourselves (or our art) too seriously. Among his works is a painting titled "Curing Hemorrhoids." It portrays Otafuku, a low-ranking courtesan, applying *moxa* to a customer's butt. The accompanying poem reads:

It seems that he has hemorrhoids—
So I give him a little bit of fire.

Being playful in the Zen arts, however, does not mean being silly, shallow, or simplistic. It means being free to use life's circumstances in a way that is joyful and whole.

Soen embodied this joyful freedom. A group of Zen students traveled to Ryutakuji temple in Mishima, Japan, to visit him in a cabin in which he had been living since his retirement. One of them related this story. For years Soen hadn't received any visitors, but this time he agreed to see the group and invited them into his cottage to have tea. Even though most of them had studied with him for many years, they were visibly self-conscious and awkward in front of their teacher. After half an hour or so of spotty conversation

and light chatter, Soen excused himself and disappeared into a room upstairs.

A few minutes later he reappeared on the balcony, his face covered with a Noh mask. He thrust his head through the banister, cocking it from side to side, as if examining the people below. He then crept down the stairs to the table and made his way around it, placing his face close to the face of each of his visitors. Everyone started giggling, then laughing loudly. Finally, after Soen examined the last person, he stepped back, ripped the mask off his face, and said, "I've taken off my mask. Now, you take off yours!"

Noh, a form of Japanese medieval theater, was traditionally practiced by the warrior class. It combines elements of dance, music, drama, and poetry. It is not technically one of the Zen arts, but rather a product of Japanese culture that was influenced by Zen. Some of the principles of the Zen aesthetic are present in Noh, particularly *yugen* or mystery. It also embodies simplicity, sparseness, and suggestiveness. Based on the belief that the deepest human sentiments cannot be conveyed by language, human emotions are expressed in poetic form, but they are cloaked, rather than set forth explicitly.

Masks, like the one that Soen used to such great effect, play a pivotal role in Noh. They are full-face masks that can produce a variety of expressions through the combination of lighting and the way the actor tilts his head. These changes simulate the shifts that happen naturally as we shift our face muscles. This lifelike changeability of the masks is legendary and they are collected and displayed as works of art.

Whether serious or playful, witty or evocative, Zen is alive because it is spontaneous. If you want to experience this spontaneity in your own life and work, don't waste your energy on judgment or reflection. *This is a good photograph, this is a bad photograph. I like this, I don't like that.* That's just the brambles, the entanglements that keep us from really getting in touch with our creative heart.

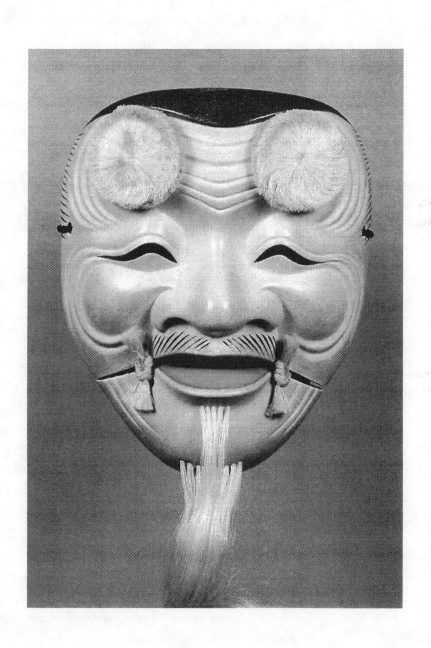

Naturalness, spontaneity, and playfulness are all aspects of the ordinary mind that catches a glimpse of the world of things just as they are. To live this life fully means to see all of it. The doorway to this experience is the creative process. Please delve deeply into it. Give it a chance to do what it is capable of doing. Engage it fully with the whole body and mind. If you do, sooner or later, this limitless way of being will be your own. It will never make sense, and you'll never be able to explain it to anybody, but you will experience it, and by so doing, you will make it real.

High is our calling, friend!
Creative Art demands the service
of a mind and heart
WILLIAM WORDSWORTH

Art Koan Practice: Express Things for What They Are

In Chapter Five we examined expressing things for what else they are. Now we will look at expressing things for what they are, which is what unequivocally characterizes the subject's uniqueness among similar objects. This difference may not be just a single characteristic. More likely, several characteristics distinguish this particular individual from the group.

It is important to not confuse the idea of the subject's uniqueness with your direct and tangible experience of it. Try to see what is actually taking place at the moment of your own interaction with the subject. Use your creative feedback group to help you see whether or not you have been successful in communicating the unique "isness" of the subject.

✳
✳
✳

ELEVEN

Mystery

Morning mist hovering in the mouth of the valley
Causes many people to miss the source.

JOHN DAIDO LOORI

The Chinese character for mystery, or yugen, is the character for mountain, which looks like an inverted letter T with two squiggles on each side of the vertical line. This line is the mountain, and the squiggles on either side represent the mist in the valley that invokes a certain anticipation of the hidden.

Mystery is usually associated with the darker side of life, with death or fear of the unknown. In religion and art, mystery is light itself. It's the lifeblood that pumps through true religious and artistic practice. Mystery is the itch that you can't scratch, the driving force of spiritual and creative journeys. It sets in motion the basic questions of our existence. It fuels genuine scientific investigation. It invites us to peek around the next corner, into the darkness.

Mystery is the seed of discovery. The term "mystical" means: "Having a spiritual meaning that is neither apparent to the senses nor obvious to the intellect. It is direct subjective communication with ultimate reality." It's the kind of communication that we can't process intellectually. We can't see it, hear it, smell it, taste it, touch it, or think it. It is very subtle and slippery, impossible to nail down or explain. Yet we're somehow aware of its presence, and it has a real impact on us.

In order for us to perceive this subtle quality, three elements must be in place: trust in our spiritual practice, trust in the creative process, and, most importantly, trust in ourselves. If any of these are missing, the whole structure collapses, and we retreat into certainty. So we trust, even if we can't explain or justify why we do what we do.

Over the years, many people have asked me why I chose to become a Zen priest. I have no idea. I can come up with all kinds of compelling explanations, but I can't articulate the real driving force that moved me in this direction. And, frankly, I don't think it's that important.

When I signed up to do Minor White's workshop at the Hotchkiss School, before being accepted for the workshop, I was required to submit personal information so an astrologer could read my chart. As a scientist of many years, I considered this ridiculous, but since I really wanted to study with Minor, I agreed.

Charlotte, the astrologer, told me that everything I was doing and would do for the next ten years was preparation for the ultimate purpose of my life's work.

"What am I going to do?" I asked.

Charlotte said, "You're going to be a high priest in a strange religion."

I burst out laughing. "Charlotte, you have no idea how wrong you are! That's impossible."

She checked the chart. "No. It's very clear." She nodded emphatically. "You're becoming a priest."

"What about photography?" I asked.

She mused, "Yes, photography will be there, but just as an aside. The major thrust is this religion. And what is actually more prominent than photography is books. You will be writing a lot of books. . . ."

I interrupted, "Books on photography?"

"No. Books on that religion."

I didn't even argue. At that time, there was no way that I could remotely imagine myself as a priest of any kind of religion. As my journey unfolded, I followed each step where it took me, all the while repeating to myself that none of it made any sense. With time, I stopped trying to make sense and just gave myself over to what lay in store for me.

Ten years later, finding and buying the property for the Zen Arts Center didn't make sense to anyone, yet I trusted my intuition. I had no money, no supportive community, and no concrete plans to speak of, yet I shook hands with the owner because a blue heron flew overhead.

Some years earlier I had been involved in a project to photograph migrating shorebirds along the East Coast flyway. For a couple of seasons, I spent several weeks following spring migrations from the Carolinas, north to Maine, photographing along the shoreline. I amassed a comprehensive collection of images, but somehow, I had been unable to get a good print of the great blue heron. I tried in all sorts of places, but this elusive and majestic bird always flew away before I could photograph it.

After numerous attempts, I finally abandoned what had turned into an obsession. I forgot about the bird. A year later, as I was driving early one morning past a pond near my house, I saw a silhouette of a blue heron standing in the shallow water. I stopped the car and watched it. The bird saw me, but didn't flush. I got out of the car and unloaded my camera and tripod. The heron watched me, seemingly unafraid. As far as I could tell, it was allowing me to be in its presence.

I began to photograph. At one point, the heron appeared to be posing, still and dignified, before my lens. I finished and bowed to it. At that instant, it flew off. After so many years of trying to photograph the shy bird, why had this particular one allowed me to

photograph it? Was it because I had let go of the expectation of getting the photograph? Or because the space around the pond was open and the heron did not feel threatened? More importantly, does it really matter? What chance does a rational justification have against the beauty and mystery of our lives?

Standing on the grounds of the Benedictine monastery I was about to purchase, the blue heron appeared again as a portent. All my friends kept telling me that I was crazy: "The only way you can save yourself from going bankrupt is to turn the place into a restaurant, a bed and breakfast, or a nightclub. Who the hell is going to come to a Zen Arts Center in Mount Tremper? Where *is* Mount Tremper, anyway?" It truly didn't make sense, but by that time I was on friendly terms with the intuitive, so I just followed what my gut was telling me to do, with no hesitations and no expectations, straight into the darkness and fruitfulness of mystery.

In the photography workshops I lead, I ask participants to go out to photograph without expectations. For most people, the moment they hear the assignment, they try to figure out exactly what they're going to photograph and how. But when we go out with an idea, we close the doors of possibility. When we expect a certain result, only two things can happen: We will either find what we're looking for or we won't. Either way, we are blind to all other possibilities because we're focused on our expectation. Don't expect, either in life or in art. Open yourself to discovery. Enjoy the mystery. All the good stuff is hidden in the dark corners. It's what gives life its sense of vitality.

The human imagination is infinitely powerful and profound. It allows each person to bring to the work of art something that is unique to him or her. Five people looking at the same painting will not see it in the same way. Yet the work of art will speak to each of them in their own language. That's the wonder of mystery.

In art, mystery is touched through understatement and implication. Mystery abhors naked exposure and explanation. In the

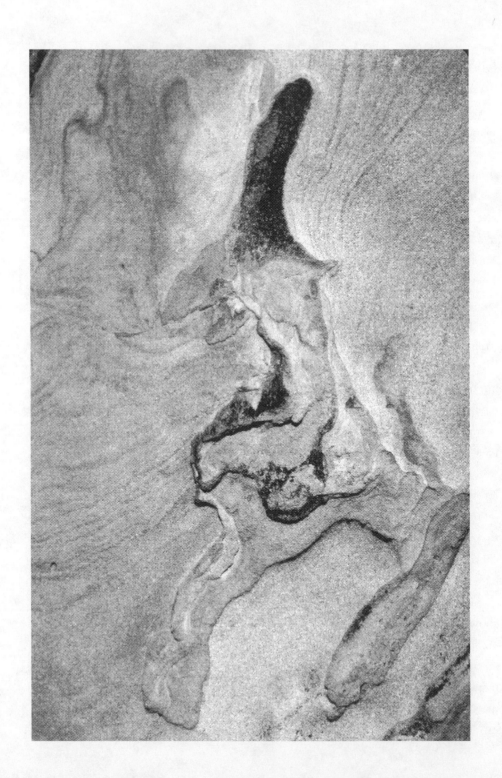

early years of cinema, many films were characterized by the qualities of understatement and implications. Film directors in those days could make your heart race with mere suggestion, letting the mind fill in the blanks. More recently, Hitchcock could horrify you with a passing shadow. By contrast, modern films blatantly strive for shock effect, turning the viewer into a voyeur, rather than an active participant. Modern war movies depict carnage, bodies disintegrating in slow motion.

A thousand-pound bow and arrow
won't hit a mouse.

JAPANESE PROVERB

In a collection of photographs and poems that Minor White produced during World War II, there are no images of the battle-front, no explicit violence, no blood or gore. Just portraits of soldiers. Yet, in them, I see more horror and sadness of war and death than in any of the graphic Associated Press wire photos and news releases that we were all being fed.

Zen art is open-ended. The *enso* or Zen circle, a symbol of enlightenment, for example, is almost always left open. The missing piece is to be supplied by the viewer. In completing the brushwork, the viewer gets involved and experiences a sense of completion in the art. Haiku only presents a glimpse, yet its emotional impact can be enormous because the reader has room to enter and create the full picture. The poet only provides the seed.

Because the message in Zen art is never spelled out, it draws you in, inviting you to probe the deeper layers of the experience.

Zen stone gardens seem very simple—just a few stones and raked gravel. But, if we take the time, the more we explore and sit with them, watching the light change, the more we see how all the elements are constantly changing, altering the infinite net of their relationships. There is always something new. Mystery is always present and waiting in every moment, at every step.

Every art has its mystery, its spiritual rhythm.

D. T. SUZUKI

In the early seventies, after Minor White's workshop and my developing interest in Zen, I moved as close to Dai Bosatsu as I could. The farmhouse I lived in with my wife and son was near the Delaware River. On the farmhouse's property stood a silo that taunted me every time I passed by, asking—begging, it seemed—to be photographed.

I started photographing it in the summer, and continued through the seasons, making sure I visited at different times of the day. I did this every day for almost two years. At the end of this time I put together a slide-sound sequence of the images, with over fifty slides showing the silo's many hidden faces, aspects that would not be easily apparent to the casual observer. Isn't this what art is about—bringing to light new and different aspects of ordinary, everyday objects?

I have favorite places to shoot, sites that are always overflowing with fresh images. One of them is on the Delaware River. I've been returning there for over forty years. It's an unremarkable stretch of flowing water with rocks. Each time I visit this place, I receive boundless gifts. They are always different. Each rock, each blade of grass, each reflection beckons. I cannot exhaust them, no matter how much I photograph.

Once, at the beginning of my Zen journey, I was shooting there when suddenly I saw a striking image and felt a powerful attraction to it. I took my time to set up the large-format camera I was carrying. After all the preparations, I made an exposure, not having any idea what it was. I repacked my camera and walked away. I hiked for a few hundred yards when I observed that my consciousness had changed somehow. I started thinking about the photograph that I had just taken, wondering if I had really seen what I thought I had. I walked back to the exact place where I stood to take the picture—the tripod marks were still in the sand—but the image wasn't there. I concluded that I had imagined it.

It wasn't until I developed the print that I saw the image again. I framed the photograph, and some time later, when I was teaching at Naropa University, a Tibetan lama happened to be visiting with me. He saw the photograph and said, "Oh! That's Avalokiteshvara Bodhisattva." To me, it looked like an abstract image of a riverbank, but I was curious and asked, "Avalokiteshvara? How do you spell that?" I looked up the name and found out that Avalokiteshvara is the bodhisattva—a kind of saint or deity—of compassion.

There is always an aspect of life, of art, of religious practice that is a little bit out of our reach. We can trust that. The three essentials of trust—trust in your spiritual practice, trust in the creative process, and trust in yourself—must ripen if we are to free ourselves. Give yourself permission to *be* yourself, and don't be frightened by the unknown.

Just as with Zen art, life is a process that is constantly unfolding. It is boundless, without edges. When we work with koans and see into them, we can always go further. Our appreciation of a koan can continuously deepen. Twenty years ago we were not ready to see what we are able to see right now. And right now we are not ready to see what will unfold for us in twenty years. Our mind is not ready to receive it, no matter how much we push and strain. That, too, is part of the mystery.

The most beautiful thing we can experience is the mysterious. It is the source of all true art and science.

ALBERT EINSTEIN

The truth is also constantly unfolding. It can't be contained. In Zen, as we practice and verify the truth in our experiences, our vision extends infinitely. Practice is ceaseless. We clarify our aspiration, we practice, realize the truth, and actualize it as our lives. Then we return to our aspiration, we practice, realize, actualize. It's a continual spiral, each sweep of the circle rising higher and higher. New perspectives, previously unseen, appear and open up. There's always a little bit further to go, always something that is yet unseen.

TWELVE

Expressing the Inexpressible

Tao cannot be conveyed by either words or silence. In that state which is neither speech nor silence, its transcendental nature may be apprehended.

ZHUANGZI

According to the Zhuangzi, the transcendental nature of reality cannot be apprehended and conveyed unless we can attain the state that is neither speech nor silence. Before we realize that state, we are dealing only with shadows, derivatives, and echoes of reality.

This chapter addresses the fundamental challenge, common to art and Zen, of expressing the inexpressible—the mystical essence of life, of this moment.

When you look, it is formless;
When you call, it echoes

FUYU

Words frequently separate us from that essence, creating illusory compartments and divisions, reflecting the dualistic aspect of our minds, yet words themselves can also be the state that is "neither speech nor silence."

Among the many artless arts that developed in close association with Zen, poetry has played and continues to play an important role in the training of both monastic and lay Zen practitioners. A student cannot get through formal Zen training without looking deeply into the function of language and developing skills for turning a phrase, creating a poem that fits an occasion and captures its spirit. In general, these poems can be categorized in three groups: poems written by an individual, poems written as an offering, and dharma words—poems written by a Zen priest or master as an expression of the teachings.

The first group, poems written by an individual, includes poems as expressions of realization, enlightenment, and death poems. Historically, poems were used by many Zen monks to express their insight or realization. Huineng was an illiterate layman living in the South of China. He became enlightened upon hearing an itinerant monk chant the *Diamond Sutra*. When the monk reached the line "You should activate the mind without dwelling on anything," Huineng experienced deep realization. Although Huineng was illiterate, a non-Buddhist, and had never heard the sutra before, this line somehow triggered his insight. He traveled north to the monk's monastery and met the abbot who immediately recognized his clarity. But because of Huineng's illiteracy and lack of education, the abbot sent him to work in the rice shed. One day, the master announced that he would like his monks to express their understanding of the dharma. He said to the community, "The truth is hard to understand. Don't uselessly memorize my words and take that as your only responsibility. Each of you should freely compose a verse. If the meaning of the words is in accord with the truth, I will transmit to you the seal of accomplishment." No one but the head monk felt up to the task. He composed a verse and posted it on the wall outside the abbot's quarters. The verse read:

The body is precisely the Bodhi tree.
The mind is like a bright mirror's stand.
Time after time, make the effort to wipe it clean.
Do not allow it to attract dust and dirt.

When Huineng heard that the head monk had composed a poem, he asked one of the monks to recite it to him. Upon hearing the poem he said, "It's not quite right." He then composed a verse of his own and asked the monk to write it for him and post it:

The root of Bodhi is not a tree.
And the bright mirror is not a stand.
Ultimately there is not a single thing.
What could attract dust and dirt?

The master of the temple recognized Huineng's poem as being "in accord with the truth" and transmitted to him the seal of accomplishment. Clearly, Huineng's illiteracy was not a handicap to expressing his profound understanding of the nature of the universe.

Sometimes poetical presentations of the dharma were challenged, not accepted, as in the following koan, where Lingyun's poem is accepted by his teacher, but not by his dharma brother:

Once, Zen Master Lingyun had realization upon seeing peach blossoms. He then wrote a poem:

For thirty years I have looked for enlightenment.
Many times leaves fell, new ones sprouted.
One glimpse of peach blossoms,
now no more doubts—just this.

He presented his understanding to Guishan. Guishan said, "One who enters the way with ripened causes will never leave. You should maintain it well."
Later Xuansha heard about it and commented, "You've got it right, senior brother. But you have not as yet achieved maintaining it."

Enlightenment poems are expressions of an individual's experience of seeing into the nature of reality. Layman Dongpo was a famous Chinese essayist who is said to have had a profound understanding of the vast ocean of Buddhism and to have been "a dragon in the sea of letters." Becoming enlightened upon hearing the sound of a stream in a mountain valley, Dongpo composed the following verse:

> The sound of the valley stream
> is exactly his broad, long tongue.
> The form of the mountain
> is nothing other than his clear, pure body.
> Through the night,
> the eighty-four thousand gathas.
> The next day,
> how can I present them to anyone?

Eighty-four thousand was said to be the number of atoms in the human body, as well as the number of manifestations of the Buddha of infinite light. Eighty-four thousand hymns, every cell in the body a hymn, and suddenly Layman Dongpo heard them. "How can I tell it to people the next day?" he wondered. When one of my students first read this story she asked me, "Isn't this the same thing that people do when they want to share their supposedly superior insight? Is he just trying to figure out how to do it?" But perhaps Dongpo did not really mean, "How can I share?" but rather, "How can I serve?"

Perhaps he was responding to the challenge of expressing the ineffable to others, the challenge of giving. Indeed, what is the point of insight if it cannot be given, shared, used in a way to nourish both ourselves and others? Isn't this the perennial question that every artist faces—indeed, every person concerned with how to live a truly meaningful life? What *is* true giving?

Master Dogen, commenting on this, said, "That night, when the poet was enlightened, can we say that the poet was enlightened by the sounds of the brook? Or was it the brook that was enlightened by the poet? Dare anyone say that this is a pint of water or an ocean into which all rivers enter? Ultimately speaking, is it the poet who has been enlightened, or is it the mountains and rivers that are enlightened?" For Dogen, mountains, rivers, and the poet are nondual, a single reality. Therefore, it is not possible to speak of either the poet as the creator of the poem, or the brook as the creator of the sound. Cause and effect have merged into a single reality.

Anticipating death and preparing to depart consciously and gracefully is part of many cultures, East and West. The question of life and death is central to Zen, and just as life is celebrated with poetry, so is death. Many accomplished practitioners, in preparation for their own death, will bathe, write a death verse, and compose themselves in zazen, then leave their bodies.

For fifty-four years encompassing the whole world
In a single leap breaking open the universe
—Just This—
This whole body lacks nothing at all.
Alive, I fall into the Yellow Springs.

EIHEI DOGEN

Zen master Ikkyu lived from 1394 to 1481. He was well known as a wild and raggedy Zen poet. Ikkyu's death poem was one of my teacher Maezumi Roshi's favorites. It reads:

I won't die.
I'm not going anywhere
I'll be here.
But don't ask me anything.
I won't answer.

Poems written as an offering include appreciatory and congrat-
ulatory verses. The following is a typical appreciatory verse offered
to a *shuso* (head monk) upon completion of a successful dharma encounter, the rite of passage from a junior to a senior status in the
community:

Holding it up
putting it down.
Wielding the double-edged sword
she cuts away the extra.
Nothing can hinder the river
in its journey to the great ocean.
Like clouds following the wind
no trace of passing remains.
Well done shuso, well done.

Liturgical poems are verses written by a Zen priest and used in
Zen liturgy, particularly during ceremonies of birth, death, funer-
als, memorials, and special holidays. The poem is integrated into the
liturgy itself and is written and presented by the officiant. It takes
the form of "dharma words," a teaching relevant to the occasion. I
offered the following poem in celebration of Buddha's birthday at
Zen Mountain Monastery in the spring of 1999:

A hundred thousand blessed lives
born in a single moment, thus!
Timeless and alone between heaven and earth
the World-honored One.

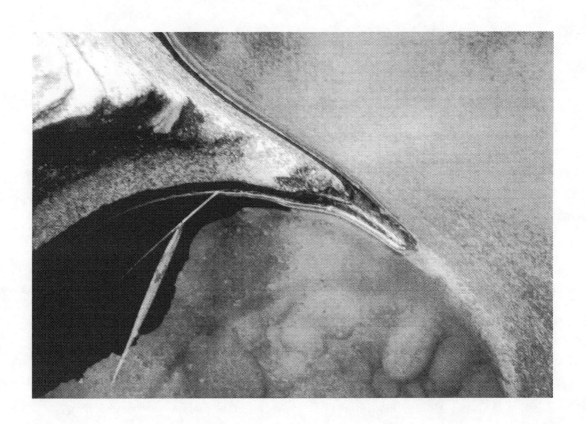

Generation after generation
Spring arrives.
What words can describe the sweet fragrance
of the ancient plum blossoms?
Ro-o-o-o!
From within the valley mist
sounds of the first morning fill the air.

The expression "Roooo!" is a sound that articulates the ineffable. Similar expressions are found in many poems where, because of the deep significance of what the officiant is attempting to say, in the end, it is manifested simply as a sound. The use of the Zen shout expresses the truth in a similar way.

Poetry is also pivotal in the study of koans. Many masters have created collections of koans that they used in training their students. In putting together these collections they would always add a verse that functioned as a pointer to assist the student in unraveling the koan. Master Dogen, in one of the volumes of the *Eihei Koroku*, offered a poem as a commentary to each koan he took up. The koan collections known as *The Gateless Gate, The Blue Cliff Record*, and *Book of Serenity*, available in English, are classic examples of the use of verses in combination with a koan. In *The Gateless Gate*, Master Wumen includes the following case:

One day a monastic asked Master Fengxue, "Both speech and silence are dualistic. How can we be free and non-transgressing?"

Fengxue responded with a verse:

How fondly I remember
Jiangnan in March—
The partridges are calling;
the flowers are fragrant.

Master Wumen added his own verse as a pointer to help understand the koan. He said:

Fengxue used no elaborate phrases.
Before the lips are even opened,
the truth is revealed.
If you keep on talking and chattering,
You will always be at a loss.

Sometimes the poem itself becomes the subject of a koan, as in the case of "Yunmen's 'You have missed it!' ":

A monastic once asked Master Yunmen, " 'The light shines serenely through the universe—' "
Yunmen interrupted, "Isn't that Zhangzhuo's poem?"
The monastic said, "Yes, it is."
Yunmen said, "You've missed it."
Later, Master Sixin said, "Tell me, why did he miss it?"

Or, the response to a koan can be poetic:

Changsha one day went for a walk into the mountains. Upon his return, the head monastic said, "Teacher, where have you been?"
Changsha said, "I've just come from wandering in the mountains."
The monk asked again. "What were you doing?"
Changsha said, "First I went following the fragrant grasses, and then I returned pursuing the falling blossoms."
The head monk said, "You seem full of springtime."
Changsha said, "It's even better than the autumn dew on the lotus leaves."

Master Yuanwu pointed out in his commentary on this koan, "The point of Changsha's wit was sharp and swift. If anyone asked about the teachings, he would then give him the teachings. If someone needed a verse, he would then give a verse."

Because of the inherent limitations of language in communicating the truth of Zen, masters of antiquity have resorted to radical ways of using language to communicate the teachings. Master Zhaozhou, Yunmen, and much later Dogen, became known for a style of teaching called "lips and mouth Zen." They often offered pithy expressions that pointed directly to the heart of the matter.

> A monk asked Yunmen, "What is the talk that goes beyond the buddhas and ancestors?"
> Yunmen said, "Cake."
>
> A monastic asked Zhaozhou, "What is the meaning of the Ancestor [Bodhidharma] coming from the West?"
> Zhaozhou said, "The cypress tree in the garden."
>
> Master Dogen was asked upon his return from China, "What did you realize?"
> Dogen said, "Eyes horizontal, nose vertical."

These very direct and practical responses to esoteric questions tend to cut off the myriad streams of thought and stun the mind, bringing it into the eternal present, which is neither the world of phenomena, nor the realm of the absolute. Endless permutations and combinations are reduced to a very pointed answer.

In his classification of koans, Master Hakuin created a group called *gonsen* koans, cases specifically directed to "the study and investigation of words." A modern master, Isshu Miura, commented on the gonsen koans in his book *The Zen Koan:* ". . . For the very reason that there are no words and phrases, words and phrases are

the more wonderful. Because the hidden valley is without partiality, it echoes the footsteps of whomsoever enters it. For the very reason that there is not a single thing, the ten thousand things are the more mysterious. Because the great bell is of itself soundless, when it is struck by the bell beam it reverberates with a flood of sound."

Another way of approaching the thing is to consider it unnamed, unnameable.

FRANCIS PONGE

These gonsen koans are word traps in which the teachings are embedded. In order to resolve them, a student must be able to pass through the entanglements created by words, beneath which the truth of the koan is hidden.

Priest Nirvana of Baizhang asked Nanquan, "Is there any dharma that has not been spoken by the sages in the past?"
Nanquan said, "It's not mind, it's not Buddha, it's not a thing."
Nirvana said, "Have you finished speaking?"
Nanquan said, "I am like this. What about you?"
Nirvana said, "I am not a teacher. How should I know if there is a dharma that has or has not been spoken?"
Nanquan said, "I don't understand."
Nirvana said, "I have said enough for you."

"Wordless" poetry outside the formal setting of Zen training was brought to its perfection in the form of haiku, where the subject is released almost as quickly as it is taken up. The poem is an opening into reality. It invites the listener to enter.

Not saying anything
Neither guest, nor host,
Nor white chrysanthemum

RYOTA

The development, refinement, and popularization of haiku was largely the work of Matsuo Basho, who was born in 1644. He became a serious student of Zen and began to travel around Japan, teaching the art of *renga,* linked verses. Basho was greatly influenced by the sense of austerity present in the poems of some of his predecessors, among them the Buddhist priest Saigyo and the poet Iio Sogi.

As Basho's style matured, so did the quality of his poems. One of the best-known haiku was written during a conversation Basho had with his Zen teacher as they were sitting in a quiet garden. The master posed the following question: "What is the reality prior to the greenness of moss?" As Basho concentrated all of his energy on the problem, he heard a noise and composed the following verse:

The ancient pond
a frog leaps in
water-sound

To carry the self forward and realize the ten thousand
dharmas is delusion. That the ten thousand dharmas
advance and realize the self is enlightenment.

EIHEI DOGEN

Basho's haiku describes an actual occurrence—an evening silence in the countryside broken by a splash. Hearing the frog leaping into the water, Basho blurted out the last two lines of the poem.

Then, he devoted some time to create the timeless sense suggested by the first line. With the poem Basho transformed haiku into a form of Zen literary art.

Basho was not actually known for haiku during his life. He called the verses that have come down *hokku* or "starting verses" that launched the longer renga he was so well recognized for. Basho said: "Hokku is simply what is happening here in this particular place at this particular moment."

To write haiku, to become this intimate with the moment, the poet must completely disengage, if only for an instant, all of her interpretive faculties. The mind must become one with the world, a detail of the world—the splash, a peach blossom, a neon sign flashing along the highway, the sound of a mountain stream. The poet's craft has to slip through the intellectual filters and instinctively record the image that has been perceived. As Basho said, "In writing, do not let a hair's breadth separate you from the subject. Speak your mind directly; go to it without wandering thoughts." For an instant, the artist opens to the ineffable truth of Zen. With the self out of the way, the world advances a step.

Basho's haiku expresses the ideal that haiku poets have since striven to attain: to share with the audience, through the medium of the written or spoken word, the essential nature of the subject at hand. In other words, to close the gap between the artist, the subject, and the audience perceiving the piece of art.

Poetry is just the evidence of life. If your life
is burning well, poetry is just the ash.

LEONARD COHEN

Poetry is also used extensively in connection with other Zen arts. Many zenga paintings incorporate within them a short text in prose or verse called *san*. San are composed either by the artist or another person as a way of deepening and clarifying the religious content of the image. Many of the classical zenga are Zen koans expressed visually and poetically. The natural environment has been the traditional subject matter for this kind of expression. It is said that a single zenga of nature, combined with san, can be the embodiment of our true self. At their best, the words and pictures say something together that neither of them can say alone.

My photography teacher Minor White experimented with combining images and words, in one case going so far as to inscribe the poem directly on the emulsion surface. For the past thirty years I have also added words to images. I have found that this format provides a dimension that is not available when either the photograph or poem appears alone, a dimension that takes the aesthetic and spiritual content a little deeper. I've always felt that painters could explore poetry, and poets could explore painting, as a way to expand their creative vision.

The challenge that Zen masters have faced for thousands of years has been how to bring to life a teaching that essentially cannot be communicated, simply because it is already present in each and every individual. Poetry and koans have been powerful tools for facilitating the awakening of this inherent reality.

PART IV

Endless Spring

Set down the baggage, take off the blinders.
See for yourself
This very place is the valley of the Endless Spring.
This very body is the body of the universe.

JOHN DAIDO LOORI

THIRTEEN

Intimate Words

In Zen, the truth that precedes sound and the intuitive perception that follows a phrase is called intimate talk—an expression that can be recognized and understood even though it has no sound. We meet these expressions with a truth that is already present within us.

Listening to shakuhachi music or the vocal improvisations of Meredith Monk, I close my eyes, lean my head back, and just let the sounds in. I am transported to a place that is familiar, yet somehow forgotten, almost primordial. I experience something that is within me that I didn't know was there. Is it the music? Is it that which precedes those sounds? Is it the intuitive understanding that follows them? Or is it all three?

Although in intimate expression there is no sound, this expression cannot be called silent. This is not a matter that can be grasped by linear, rational, dualistic thinking, thinking that sets up polarities and oppositions: good against bad, heaven against earth, self against other, form against emptiness, speech against silence. Intimacy is not a matter that exists in the realm of polarities. Intimacy is the place where opposites merge.

Just as sound contains not-sound, so, too, does form contain not-form. Each is unified in a single, ineffable reality—right here, right now. Spirit and matter are the same reality. There's not some special spiritual force that exists separate from the phrases we utter or the forms we perceive.

Ordinary understanding is seeing with the eye and hearing with the ear. Intimacy is seeing with the ear and hearing with the eye.

On Mount Gridhrakuta, the Buddha addressed an assembly of thousands. He didn't say a word. He picked up a flower and held it up for everybody to see. Out of the entire assembly, only Mahakashyapa, one of his disciples, smiled. Noticing Mahakashyapa's smile, the Buddha said, "I have the all-pervading truth, the exquisite teaching of formless form. It has no reliance on words and letters. I now hand it over to Mahakashyapa." Among the Zen koans, this is an archetypal example of intimate speech.

> The Buddha gave an intimate discourse,
> Mahakashyapa did not conceal it.
> Flowers open in a night of falling rain,
> Valley streams at dawn fill with spring fragrance.

Do not mistake the calling and answering of our regular conversations as intimate talk. The calling and the answering are ripples on the surface. They are not the intimate talk itself. In intimate talk no communication whatsoever can take place. Communication requires two points. Something goes from A to B. In intimacy, there are not two distinct entities and nothing to go from A to B. In the Zen transmission of wisdom nothing is transmitted; nothing goes from teacher to student. The student already has what the teacher

Intimate Words

225

has. The student already is the teacher. You already have what the enlightened one has. It just needs to be awakened, brought to life. Intimate talk brings it to life.

The best we can do is be always open and receptive. Whether we're receiving Zen teachings, a work of art, or life itself, we can let it in, taste it, experience it, let it penetrate our cells, our pores, our breath, our being, and then leave it be.

In intimacy, there's no knowing. There's no reference system from which to know. There's no outside or inside. There's no thing that can be known or person that can know it. Not knowing fills the universe. There's no place to put this gigantic body. It contains everything.

Without looking out the window
you can see the way of heaven.

LAOZI

Dogen said, "Life is nothing more than searching for and acting out the myriad possibilities of meaning with which the self and the world are pregnant." We do this through expressions and activities. This involves not only the human world, but the nonhuman and nonliving worlds. Sit openly in the presence of a tree. Is nothing happening? Sit with an immobile and mute rock. Is nothing communicated?

All of reality is always awake and transmitting the truth, pointing to the truth. Even the insentient transmit intimate words. These mountains and rivers themselves are continually manifesting the words of the buddhas and ancient teachers. Dogen calls the sounds of the valley streams the eighty-four thousand hymns. The sounds of

the river and the form of the mountain are all expressions of the buddha nature in absolute emptiness.

Silently and serenely one forgets all words.
Clearly and vividly, it appears before you.
When one realizes it, it is vast and without edges.

HONGZHI ZHENGJUE

In the opening words of the "Mountains and Rivers Sutra," Dogen says, "These mountains and rivers of the present are the actualization of the word of ancient buddhas." Some translations use "way" instead of "word." I think "word" is more appropriate because Dogen specifically calls this chapter a sutra—the words of the Buddha. Rocks, trees, the wind, the ocean, are constantly manifesting the dharma.

Indeed, if we examine this teaching carefully, we see that all of the phenomena of this great universe—audible, inaudible, tangible and intangible, conscious and unconscious—are constantly expressing the truth of the universe. Do you hear it? Can you see it? If not, then heed the instructions of Master Dongshan and "see with the ear, listen with the eye." Only then will you understand the ineffable reality of the world.

In his poem "The Jewelled Mirror of Samadhi," Master Dongshan attempted to describe suchness, this-very-moment-as-it-is, in all its perfection and completeness, using many beautiful metaphors to convey this instant of reality. In one of the lines of the verse, he exclaims, "baba wawa." When I first read this I had no idea what it meant, so I asked Maezumi Roshi. He said that it was the cooing of an infant. That cooing is the poignant expression of this incredible truth, of the buddha nature itself. It's no different than the song of a bird, the sound of the wind in the pine trees, a Zen master's shout, or Buddha silently holding up a flower on Mount Gridhrakuta.

Something must have been manifested when Buddha raised the flower because Mahakashyapa got it. It wasn't until after Mahakashyapa had gotten it and smiled that the Buddha announced for the benefit of the rest of the assembly, "I have the all-pervading truth, the exquisite teaching of formless form. It has no reliance on words and letters. I now hand it over to Mahakashyapa." First, Buddha held up a flower and blinked his eyes, Mahakashyapa smiled and the transmission was complete. Then, after that fact, the announcement was made.

Not equal to
Not metaphor
Not standing for
Not sign.

MINOR WHITE

Many times during my training, I sat in front of my teacher in dokusan, on the edge of seeing something. I would ask him and wait for an answer. But he gave me nothing: not a smile, not a twinkle in his eye, not a snort, not a quiver, and yet BAM! I would see it; I would get it. I repeatedly witness this as I am working with my students, in art and in Zen. I point or stay silent. Their realizations emerge from within. That's why we call realization "the wisdom that has no teacher." Everything is already in you. When you are open and receptive in your asking, when you're alive and alert, everything is constantly teaching, everything is constantly

nourishing. Direct pointing and intimate words are devices that awaken that which is already there.

Think about the stillness, then the sound, and then the perception that follows. Nothing comes from the outside. It's like the koan. When you really see a koan clearly, nothing has come in from the outside. A good teacher tries to avoid derailing the process of discovery that the student can experience. When students discover it for themselves, they own it.

The truth is what happens in each one of us. That's the cardinal point of practice. Practice, whether Zen or art, is a way of making the invisible visible. We are all complete, lacking absolutely nothing. This was the first teaching of the Buddha. It remains the first teaching of Zen. Some may realize the truth of this perfection, some may not, but nevertheless, we are all perfect. Practice is a way of making that fact visible.

This experience of intimate communication can take place when art is functioning at its best, when life is lived most freely and completely. The more this happens, the more easily new vistas begin to open and we begin to realize that the seemingly "mystical" experience is actually something quite ordinary. It is part of your life and my life. And indeed, an ordinary aspect of all beings.

FOURTEEN

Indra's Net

Imagine, if you will, a universe in which all things have a mutual identity. They all have an interdependent origination: When one thing arises, all things arise simultaneously. And everything has a mutual causality: What happens to one thing happens to the entire universe.

Imagine a universe that is a self-creating, self-maintaining, and self-defining organism—a universe in which all its parts and the totality are a single entity, all of the pieces and the whole thing are, at once, one thing.

This description of reality is not a holistic hypothesis or an all-encompassing idealistic dream. It is your life and my life. The life of the mountain and the life of the river. The life of a blade of grass, a spiderweb, the Brooklyn Bridge. These things are not related to each other. They're not part of the same thing. They're not similar. Rather, they are identical to each other in every respect.

Lest we assume that this is simply some esoteric Buddhist meta-physics, consider the recent quantum physics experiment conducted in Geneva, Switzerland. The researchers took a pair of photons and sent them along optical fibers in opposite directions to sensors in two villages north and south of Geneva. Reaching the ends of the fibers, the photons were forced to make a random choice between alternative and equally possible pathways. Since it is expected that there is no way for the photons to communicate with each other, classical physics predicted that one photon's choice of a path would have no relationship or effect on the other photon's choice. But when the results were studied, the independent decisions by the pairs of photons always matched and complemented each other exactly, even though there was no physical way for them to relay information back and forth. If there was communication, it would have had to exceed the speed of light, which, according to Einstein, is not possible.

There is no place at all that is not looking at you.

RAINER MARIA RILKE

Each photon knew what was happening to its distant twin and mirrored the twin's response. This took place in less than one one-thousandth of the time a light beam would have needed to carry the news from one place to the other. The connection and correlation between the two particles were instantaneous. They were behaving as if they were one reality. This experiment indicates that long-range connections exist between quantum events, and that these connections do not rely on any physical media. The connections are immediate and reach from one end of the universe to the other. Spatial distance does not interfere or diminish the connectedness of the events.

This interconnectedness of all things revealed in the Geneva experiment has been part of the Zen teachings for 1,500 years. It's spoken of as the diamond net of Indra, in which all things are interconnected, co-arising, sharing mutual causality. Every connection in this net is a diamond with many facets, and each diamond reflects every other diamond in the net. In effect, this means that each diamond contains every other diamond. You cannot move one diamond without affecting all the others. And the whole net extends throughout all space and time.

Only the incomprehensible gives any light.

SAUL BELLOW

This diamond net is not a metaphor. For Zen Buddhists, it is an accurate description of reality. It is a description of what is realized in the practice of Zen. That is, the fact that we are all totally, completely, and intricately interconnected throughout time and space.

This same truth was expressed by the Indian monk Bodhidharma. As I mentioned before, Bodhidharma defined Zen as "a special transmission outside the scriptures, with no reliance on words and letters. A direct pointing to the human mind and the realization of enlightenment."

One of the immediate misconceptions about this statement is to devalue words or imagine that by remaining mute we arrive at enlightenment, that ideas have no value in realizing the truth of the universe. There are Zen monasteries and centers where reading is strictly forbidden and books are kept under lock and key.

Because of Bodhidharma's declaration, there evolved in Zen lore the phrase, "Painted cakes do not satisfy hunger." This is an echo of "Zen does not rely on words and letters." That is, painted cakes—a representation of reality, the words, ideas, images that describe a reality—are not the reality itself. And they do not satisfy our hunger for reality.

This is a narrow interpretation of Bodhidharma's phrase. Zen master Dogen corrected this misunderstanding. He was not only

open to using language as a way of teaching the truth of reality, but also clearly recognized that the symbol—the word or image—and the symbolized are in actual fact a single reality. Dogen took up "painted cakes" and made them nutritious. He said, "Painted cakes *do* satisfy hunger. Aside from painted cakes, there is no other way to satisfy hunger."

My photographs are painted cakes. My poems are painted cakes. This book is a painted cake. Aside from painted cakes, there is no other way to communicate what I am feeling, what I am thinking.

Artistic creations are no less real than reality. From Dogen's perspective, they are not an abstraction of reality. They are indeed reality itself. Your poems, your art, are reality. What Dogen is saying is that we need to get past our dualistic perception of the universe and the self. We need to train ourselves not to accept either the imaginings or reality at the expense of one another. They are, in fact, nondual and a clear expression of the truth.

Reality is nondual. When we are awake, all dualities—self and other, is and is not, good and bad—merge into a single suchness of the moment. They are no longer seen in the realm of this and that, the realm of separation. All the permutations and combinations that we go through in defining things always ultimately come down to right here, right now, right where you stand.

What you are looking for is who is looking.

ST. FRANCIS OF ASSISI

Yet, when we first come in contact with spiritual practice, we approach it from a deeply ingrained dualistic perspective. We perceive our whole universe in a dualistic way. Our philosophy, education, medicine, psychology, and politics are dualistic. The way we've structured the universe in our minds, the way we understand things is always from a conditioned dualistic perspective. Within that conditioning, our art is also dualistic. It is about self and other, subject and object, artist and audience.

The most powerful medicine for our dualism is to uncover the still point resting within all the dualities. This is the work that takes us past the separations and conditioning to the very ground of being. When we really make contact with the still point, we make contact with the core teaching of Zen. As we've seen before, the *Heart Sutra* refers to it as the experience of "no eye, ear, nose, tongue, body, mind; no color, sound, smell, taste, touch, phenomena; no realm of sight, no realm of consciousness." All the myriad forms dissolve.

But now, what we have is a useless lump of meat sitting on a meditation cushion. It doesn't see, it doesn't hear, it doesn't think, it doesn't love, it doesn't hate, it doesn't dance, it doesn't cry. It just sits there like a big blob of protoplasm. Is that what our life is? Is that the still point? Definitely not! Consider the life of Soen Roshi, or any of the Zen teachers introduced in this book. They were full of life, constantly manifesting life. So there must be something more, something that goes beyond that place of no eye, ear, nose, tongue, body, mind. We need to see and live beyond the quietism of the still point.

And so the process continues. We come down from the holy peak into the world. Again, the *Heart Sutra* states: "Form is no other than emptiness; emptiness is no other than form; form is exactly emptiness, emptiness exactly form." Having let go of the absolute perspective, the two apparent dualities are now merged in one reality. When mind and objects are a single reality, all dualities merge. You and I are the same thing. But I'm not you and you're not me. Both of these facts exist simultaneously. Both of these facts are true.

This truth was expressed by the ancient master Shitou Xiqian in his liturgical poem "The Merging of Differences," in which he said:

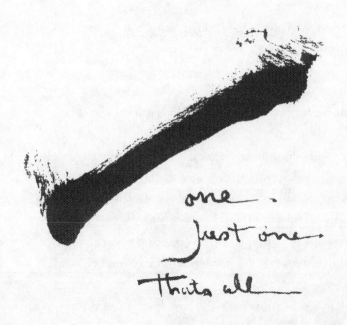

one...
just one.
That's all

Each and all, the subjective and objective
Spheres are related
And at the same time independent.
Related and yet working differently,
Though each keeps its own place . . .

. . . Within light there is darkness,
But do not try to understand that darkness.
Within darkness there is light,
But do not look for that light.
Light and darkness are a pair,
Like the foot before and the foot behind in walking.
Each thing has its own intrinsic value
And is related to everything else in function and position.
Ordinary life fits the absolute as a box and its lid.
The absolute works together with the relative
Like two arrows meeting in midair.

It's hard to get a handle on this description of reality. It is a fundamental paradox of our lives, one that is impossible to resolve intellectually—but it doesn't have to be. It simply needs to be manifested in our lives.

Do I contradict myself?
Very well then I contradict myself,
I am large, I contain the multitudes.

WALT WHITMAN

That's why practice is so important. The essence of our lives, the heart of the matter is essentially ineffable. You'll never be able to explain it. No teacher will ever be able to explain it. The Buddha could never explain it. Why? Because it doesn't come from the outside, from a Buddha or a master, a book or a phrase. It already resides in you. It's already your life. The problem is that it's obscured, buried under layers of conditioning, under habitual ways of using our minds.

In the depths of stillness all words melt away,
clouds disperse and it vividly appears before you.

JOHN DAIDO LOORI

What's being offered in all the incredible teaching of Zen and the Zen arts is simply a process. If you walk away from this book thinking you understand Zen or creativity, then I have failed. If everything goes well, you will never understand it. On the other hand, if you can appreciate the process and are willing to engage it, you will have a way to return to your inherent perfection, the intrinsic wisdom of your life.

Illustrations

134 Torei Enji (1721–1792). *Enso.* Sumi-e on paper, 12⅜ × 21¾″, The Gitter Collection

136 Muchi (Late 13th Century). *Bird on an Old Pine,* Sumi-e on paper, 31¼ × 15¼″, Private collection

138 Yamaoka Tesshu (1836–1888). *Dragon.* Sumi-e on paper, 17½ × 23¾″, The Gitter Collection

143 Taizan Maezumi. *Thus!* 1981. Sumi-e on paper, 24 × 33½″, ZMM Archives

149 Takeda Kizaemon (owner—early 17th century). *Kizaemon Tea Bowl.* Black-and-white photograph, 3¼ × 6½, 2″ foot, Daitokuji, Kyoto

156 *Zen Garden.* Black-and-white print, 8 × 8″, ZMM Archives

159 John Daido Loori. *Oryoki Bowl,* 1990. Black-and-white photograph, 4 × 6″, ZMM Archives

164 Muchi (Late 13th century). *Persimmons.* Sumi-e on paper, 14 × 13⅛″, Ryokoin, Daitokuji, Tokyo

165 Otagaki Rengetsu. *Dried Persimmons,* 1868. Sumi-e on paper, 6¾ × 6″, New Orleans Museum of Art: Anonymous Gift, 77.83

172 Gyokusei Jikihara. *Riding the Ox,* 1982. Sumi-e on paper, 14¾ × 17⅝″, ZMM Archives

175 John Daido Loori. *Feh! 2000.* Sumi-e on paper, 2⅜ × 14″, ZMM Archives

177 John Daido Loori. *Crow,* 1997. Black-and-white photograph, 6 × 9¼″, ZMM Archives

180 Gyokusei Jikihara. *Hanshan and Shide,* 1991. Sumi-e on paper, 17¾ × 12½″, ZMM Archives

184 Sosan Genkyo (1799–1868). *Daito Kokushi.* Sumi-e on paper, 39¼ × 12″, The Gitter Collection

187 Hakuin Enkaku (1685–1769). *Curing Hemorrhoids.* Ink and color on paper, 22 × 25¼″, Eisei Bunko Museum, Tokyo

JOHN DAIDO LOORI was one of the West's leading Zen masters. He was the founder and spiritual leader of the Mountains and Rivers Order of Zen Buddhism and abbot of Zen Mountain Monastery, one of America's major Zen training monasteries.

Loori was a lineage holder in both the Rinzai and Soto Schools of Zen. Devoted to maintaining the authenticity of these traditions, Loori was known for his unique adaptation of traditional Buddhism into an American context, particularly with regard to the arts, the environment, social action, and the use of modern media as a vehicle of spiritual training and social change.

Loori was also an award-winning photographer and videographer, with a successful career in both commercial and art photography. He had over one hundred one-person and group shows both in the United States and abroad, and his photographs were published in leading photography magazines, including *Aperture* and *Time Life*.

Among Loori's seventeen publications are the upcoming *Timeless Inquiry: Master Dogen's Three Hundred Koan Shobogenzo* (Shambhala 2005), *Sitting with Koans* (Wisdom Publications, 2005), and *Teachings of the Insentient: Point Lobos Photographs* (Dharma Communications, 2004). Other titles include: *The Eight Gates of Zen* (Shambhala, 2002), *The Art of Just Sitting* (Wisdom Publications, 2002), and *The Heart of Being: Moral and Ethical Teachings of Zen* (Charles E. Tuttle, 1996). Loori contributed to a number of anthologies, and he lectured at universities and Zen centers in the United States and abroad. He died in 2009.

ABOUT THE TYPE

This book was set in Perpetua, a typeface designed by the English artist Eric Gill, and cut by The Monotype Corporation between 1928 and 1930. Perpetua is a contemporary face of original design, without any direct historical antecedents. The shapes of the roman letters are derived from the techniques of stone-cutting. The larger display sizes are extremely elegant and form a most distinguished series of inscriptional letters.

Printed in the United States
by Baker & Taylor Publisher Services